The Magick of Healing

The Magick of
Healing

KaSandra Turner

Written and illustrated by KaSandra Turner

ISBN: 979-8-9904478-2-0

CopyrightDepot.com number: 00088587-1

Author, cover art, design, and illustrations: KaSandra Turner ©.

Websites and social media:

MAGICK OF EDEN Apothecary & Intuitive Services: Herbs, Ritual Oils, and more spiritual essentials at kasandraturner.com/magickofeden
Instagram: @magickofeden

Other Works by KaSandra Turner:

Eden: Reclaiming Your Divinity through Poetry and Self-Expression

An obsession that reveals my passions
The phone that keeps on ringing
A mission I could never fail
-Poetry

To the lights that shine in my darkest hours
To the hands that help me nurture my flowers
Here is my heart, an offering to you

Book of Contents

The Suffering

How it Starts

It sometimes starts with
eyes dancing in a ring of star clusters
with sensual songs seducing sacred skins
and fingers bending against
silent stories hidden
in screaming scars

It sometimes starts with
smiles in unison
swiftly smothered with
unforgiving confusion
With minds entangled
in tainted illusions
of separation
and cynical delusions

It sometimes starts with
two halves as a whole
One clings and holds
while the other pleads to go
Sometimes the ego's strength
grows at weeds speed
consumes unkempt dreams
and leaves broken bones

KaSandra Turner

I'd Rather Not Say

Trauma turned to swords and blades
invade and pierce the lining of my cheeks
My vocal cords are clogged and reek
with the rot and mold
from thoughts during last winter
I swallow my tongue and force it down
into my belly ballooned with eternal doom

They staple their eyes shut
and dream of caricatures depicting
the masks of my misperceived truths
They become tickled with derangement
and my engagement is often shooed
An unwanted fly soaring over their food
they thought of me

I find comfort in the haunting of spirits
costumed and disguised
as the wavering parts of me
The parts that simply search
for a soothing rub
I'd rather cement my lips
and ordain silence
the advocate for my fear
Reflections of their judgments
parade my dreams
I'd rather my thoughts slumber
in the peace of my chaos

Have You Ever?

Have you ever just felt
your face ache with filth
your eyes set low
with your nose flared
as you marinate in the memory
of everything you were
and weren't for them?
Have you ever blamed yourself
because they refused to heal?
Have you ever paid another's debt
through your screams, pleads
and please don'ts?

Somewhere on the Other Side

Discovering uncomfortable truths
can sometimes be a path to lonely shadows
if that's all we can perceive
I tried my best to believe
that you meant well
That you would never engrave
your memories on my skin
I know deep within the bones of me
you just needed ease and release
You found salvation in my detriments and destruction
And now I'm beyond the shadows
howling as my echoed cries spiral into oblivion
You can call this place grief
You may call it lonely
I call it the other side of the void

I can't turn down the noise
or the voices of my vices
cause the prices you paid for my trust
was dishonesty and disappointment
I'm indebted with cleaning
the gunk you spilled
that trailed into my peace
I could've let your traumas be the hounds
that devoured you
Instead, I stayed
and prayed for you in your darkest hours

My stomach boils acid

as I rot in the memory
of your eyes of plastic
You are the true embodiment of a fracture
clayed by palms that gift malevolence
You stole the show with your lies
You wore euphemisms as cloaks of camouflage
I starve to watch you bleed
I'm desperate for pardon from my own demise
lurked in the back of your mind
when you declared your love for me

I can't return to love right now
I'm dancing with your demons on a checkered plane
Raging insane with a vacant core
Torture comforts me as I dance to your evil
I've fallen in love with hate
My body chains my soul to chaos
as I await redemption
You won't find me
if you search with those plastic eyes
I'm somewhere
on the other side of the void

Deluded.
Destroyed.
Disconnected.
Discontent.
Disgusted.
Disharmonized.
Dehumanized.

-Desperately done

Frightened and fevered
I watch my worth wither on
hindered and helpless.

KaSandra Turner

I woke up chained to a bed
with my fears clawing at the foot board
Their sharp and pointed nails
caressed those yelling metal rails
Their sparks lit a fire to my olive-green sheets
The heat of my grief made its way to my feet
and the smoke of my insecurities
replaced the air in my lungs
Behind it trailed thick blackened mucus
I couldn't cough up
The screams I could not sing
left bruises in my throat
My doubts left ten-degree burns
on my boiled skin that I failed to soothe
Grief was the pillow that soaked the sorrow
from my eyes until they dried
and left raisins below my brows
I was cooking alive while my doubts, fears and screams
formed a trine and danced around this levitating bed
Their power of three weighed me down towards hell
I was submerged in these eternal flames
To my surprise,
the fires did not completely consume me
The cackling seemed to rage infinitely
Endless cries of gasoline fed this fire

-Why is it not done with me?

The Magick of Healing

I stared through myself in the dirty mirror
I forgot to clean yesterday
when my body and mind were rivals
Dishes formed ladders that led to my ceiling
when the depression burst in laughing
I searched for my children only to find them
climbing like ivies up the walls in the living room
My desire to eat eagerly escaped
three days ago along with the sunshine
Death
grief
anger
filled the pool of my chest
I was captured by death
and she placed me in a body bag
with my body breathing
I drove across the country
with my sister sewed to my side
to live out my dreams
Yet, somehow it just feels like
I traded my family
for disappointment and loneliness
Awkwardness conceals my attempts to connect
I'm avoided by other mothers
for reasons I cannot comprehend
I bet on myself to make things better
and somehow I've convinced myself
that despite my efforts
to thrive after my husband's death
I'm still a failure with nothing to search for
So, I walk with my eyes

tracing the concrete
to avoid the reality
of being a worthless failure

You Were

You were
a sculptor evading linear time with clay
painted on their palms perfecting their craft.

You were
 a gardener planting flowers and fruit
on ten acres of land by barren hand.

You were
a cliff confident and sturdy with peace
receiving roaring currents and ocean tides.

You were
a cup of cool crisp cucumbers, mint, and Granny Smith
juiced and smothered in sweetener and ice in July.

You were
citrus squeezed from bursting oranges
organic and fresh from my grandma's tree.

You were
a soothing, still, and silent reflection
exposing the microscopic cells of my soul.

You were
a spared breath after death and misfortune,
another chance to rewrite karma.

You were

fallen feathers from angels floating
and finding their way to my lap in April.

You are
the one I mourn in the mornings
while cold, quivering, and lonely.

You are
a soul who transcended this life
as I hopelessly journey back to you.

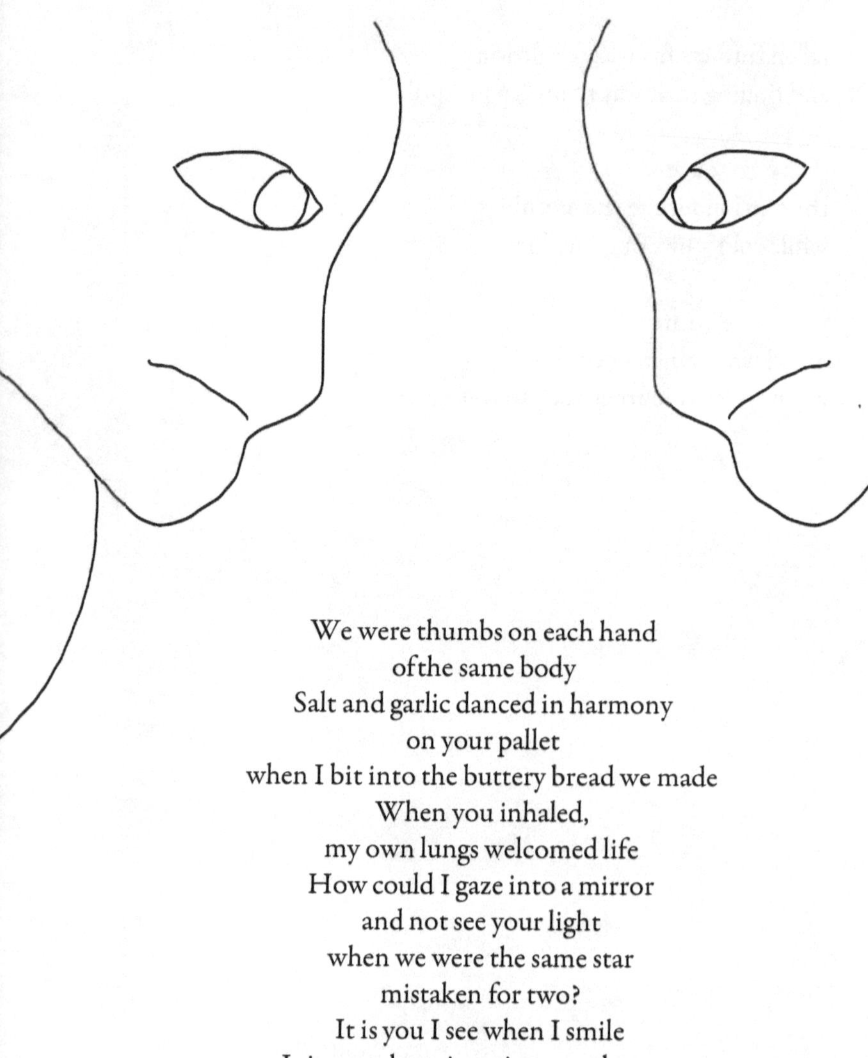

We were thumbs on each hand
of the same body
Salt and garlic danced in harmony
on your pallet
when I bit into the buttery bread we made
When you inhaled,
my own lungs welcomed life
How could I gaze into a mirror
and not see your light
when we were the same star
mistaken for two?
It is you I see when I smile
It is me who grieves in your absence

Life was fulfilling with you here.
Bright neon rainbows have turned stale and gray.

The stars have simmered quiet. The trees sway to melancholic
singing waves. The winds howl hurtful songs of sadness and
suffering.

Life is frizzled and foggy. My eyes have dried and blinked to dust.
-I'm left to nothing.

Necromancy calls me at 3am. Time travel sounds lavishing most
days. *-What are days again?*

I find myself wearing your black and grey striped shirt. I had to wash
the salt from my tears out. The one with the bleach stains on the
right chest pocket. I lost your scent. I'll never smell you again.
-I'm torn.

Missing Him

Some things I miss most
are his lips whispering his secrets
atop my breasts
His tongue telling testimonies
and victories over his triumphs
between me
beneath me
His hands were rubbered
with his warrior work ethic
yet soft enough
to make my skin sing songs
of seductive cries
He was bold
The sun envied his courage
He was a force,
a frequency that shifted and heighted
the ceiling of any room he entered
He cared deeply
Apathy never stood a chance
against the bravery
of his compassion and empathy
He was a softer tone
of divine masculine energy
He was ruthlessly kind
and rooted in an essence
of unconditional love
He never made me choose
not once or twice

KaSandra Turner

I see him through
the laughter of our two boys
They are splitting images of his soul
I miss us most
and I'll never get that back

I'd Rather it Were Me

I am unaccustomed to this existence
void of the light bared by
the charm of your sparkle
The drum of my pulse grows weakened
my blood frenzied
my mind frizzled, fragmented and filled
with the memory of your departure
These eyes that witnessed the mark of your kindness
sharpen in sight of the stories told
through the embrace you extended
to those around
I've lost my spark and grief I've found

Dazed, distraught and sterilized
I've grown incapable of baring fruit
that energizes and heats
the body I use to weave through space and time
I was betrayed by my intuition
I felt you'd leave before me
A hammer to a head unexpectedly
Intuition failed to prepare me
for that moment I seen your body pulseless and cold
The sickness that scavenged the insides of you
was patented by those in control
You were a victim of a weaponized sickness against
the masses of humanity

I'd drink hellfire
wipe my memory clean

and replay the simulation where you die
I'd do it ten times infinity cubed
if it means I'd be the one who suffers

The deacons would call us to Sunday school at 9:00am.
They'd separate us; I was seven and you were ten.
Didn't they know that socks come as a pair?
We would meet afterwards and laugh the boredom out the dusty pews.
The best part of my Sunday risings was laughing with you.

KaSandra Turner

When Robert Left

I lay here paralyzed
My back against the cold sweat seeping
through my sorrowed blankets
The echoes of your absence
invade the parts of my mind
filled with the memories
of those blazing brown eyes of yours
Well, eyes you had
Each time my eyes meet the ceiling fan
I'm held captive in that whirlpool of screams
that crawled from the pits of my insides
the day you met your demise
The day I watched you perish and pass
leaving behind the body I once made love to
Widowed at twenty-eight
the strength I conjured all these years
collapsed and sent the structure of my will
spiraling down roots of destruction
My heart became a graveyard
filled with fragmented ghosts
who haunt and whisper songs of your departure
They sing in your silence

What a gift to have married the friend
I played with as a seven-year-old child
My kinky curls caressing the plump of my cheeks
You always had that cheesy smile
with eyes tighter than tied converse shoestrings
riding on a scooter to the edge of the cosmos

The Magick of Healing

You always had a laugh that fills a room
with an angelic ring rippling in the in between
You always had a heart that was bold courageous
and kind
You embodied the divine
authentically in its purest form
without regret or shame, my Aries baby
Lately without the caress of your fingertips
seducing my earthy skin
I am bent and bruised at the knees
of the uncomfortable truth
that I have leveled eyes with my greatest suffering
The numbness that comes with knowing
that my childhood sweetheart
my husband, my king is with me in spirit
gifts me shivering shoulders iced with the trauma
of seeing the life flee from your eyes
when they rolled to the back of your mind
I'd rather swallow acid than adapt to your absence
I'd rather my stomach run rancid
If it means a seat next to you

I used to say,
I pray that you go before me
because I'd rather deal with the burden
of losing you
At least you'll be at peace
You always thought we had more time
But time as we know truly does not exist
All that exists is this moment and each moment
I spent oceans deep in the abyss of our love

KaSandra Turner

In our wisdom
In our truth
You used to ask,
What will it take for you
to step into the power of the woman
I know you are
Your beauty defies logical understanding
You are A soul connected to cosmic energy
It is an honor for art to be depicted through you
You lead my spirit closer to galaxies
You have discovered spaces no one has dared to see
You show me spectrums of light
that cannot be seen in this dimension
yet you still don't see
that the love within me is in you
What will it take for you to see
that part of your purpose
is to exist as a divine being?

As I descend into the dreams of our dates
and the reality that I couldn't save you
I willingly release anger and defeat
I surrender to the knowing
that your death was the doorway
to my purpose
You see, I learned that death is the spirit
that guides the soul into another dimension of life
Although I pour my thoughts through my tears at night
I am grateful for having seen
divinity a fingertip away

The Magick of Healing

There is so much beauty expressed in this pain
This clawing pain,
this loving suffering is a gateway
to nirvana and heaven's gates
This, to me is part of a greater plan
meant to guide us home
It is a first-class ticket
to the shores of self-love and fulfillment

I choose to set my soul on fire
with forgiveness and the knowing
that this unraveling sealed the bond between me
and my highest version
I have you to thank, my love
And at the moment
when I'm in alignment and reach enlightenment
I'll see you again
and we'll rejoice when I return home

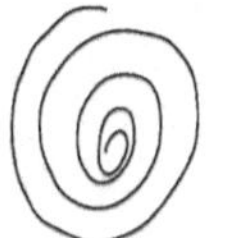

Love,

I managed to grow wings that extended beyond the sun himself when we were in the deepest abyss of our hearts together. I found the truest treasures revealed in your eyes. When God gifted you your halo, I fell into the most daunting depression that deemed my soul unworthy of freedom. Vines of confusion, anger, rage and sorrow entangle me in the tar of memories that replay in my mind. We didn't have much time; we met when I wore pigtails, ballies and barrettes in my kinky hair. Remember those heart shaped beads I wore when I got my hair braided? You think you have forever in flesh when you're seven. Reality hits you harder than a bat to a softball when you age.

I remember back in 2014 when my spiritual journey grew intense. I started really working to enhance my intuition and psychic abilities. Prayers, mantras, studies, and intuitive exercises all helped me to tap into my power as a witch. My ego put up a ferocious fight and I often feared my own power and the accuracy of my prophecies. I remember you always being there to remind me of my truest potential. A pinch of pollen falling onto my lap on a breezy spring day is the vibe your words gave. So gentle, angelic, and kind you were. I spent all that time developing my gifts to be betrayed later.

The evening when the moon grew crescent, I stopped gazed and tranced in my tracks. Time evaded my reality. My gut churned my insides to stone. I had the most "random" thought that you'd go before I would. I tried to redirect my energy to other thoughts, but the feeling persistently planted itself in my psyche. I refrained from

  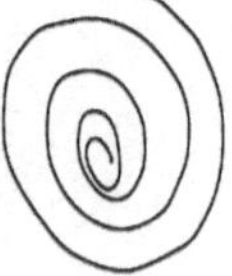

telling you this because telling you didn't feel right either. At this point along my journey my dreams, downloads, and visions always played out in real time in the future. I couldn't stomach losing you. I continued to show up for you in the best ways I could. The I love you's grew louder. The hugs grew stronger, and the laughter rang longer. The image of you transcending this human experience before me implanted itself to the most vulnerable parts of me. It was the devil to my left shoulder.

Although I never told you that I knew of this truth, I showed up and loved you as hard as I could. I would always tell you that I hope you you'd go before I do. That I'd rather be the one to suffer from losing you. I'd bear that burden if it means you'd be free of pain. I'd do it again. And again. And again, for the rest of my lives as long as it means you'd be free of suffering. I can't linguistically describe the mountain in my chest I feel. Blades, knives, and needles plague my lungs each time I attempt to breathe. I don't want to breathe at all sometimes. I'm lost without you. I love and miss you. I'll get back to crying now.

With a sorrow filled heart,

Kass

When the clouds grow gray and angry in winter
and threaten to release its tears upon the earth
you look up in awe or retreat
For this process must take place
for the sake of fruit to grow again

When thunder roars and lightening climbs
through your windows on untamed days
you surrender and respect this natural occurrence
For this is a part of a wondrous world
dancing in duality to make evens way

Your suffering may lead you
to the uncontrollable chaos
of the thoughts you cannot escape
Surrender and honor yourself
as you do for what naturally occurs

Fear filled the livingroom minutes before my mother slumped and hunched through the door. The TV and I would freeze dead like possums escaping fox claws. She carried the burdens and baggage of her customers under her eyes. I think she prayed for the end sometimes.

Fear would respond before my heart could sing empathy. She needed us to say, *I love you. Here, Momma let me take that bag.* Every grocery item she scanned totaled the number of times we found ourselves scavenging for safety some evenings she crawled in from work. We dreaded the trouble that came with her troubles.

We were drunk, drugged, and pumped with fear when all she needed was an ear. We were so busy flying afraid that we forgot to show love. We were sometimes so consumed with trauma that we forgot to be her kids. How defeated she must have felt when we confused her tiredness for anger.

KaSandra Turner

Softball

The pitcher, whose breath blends with the winds
inhales silently. She stands with her chest stoic and mighty.
She watches the batter to calculate the throw.
       Her glares glow and she stings me with her irritation.
The pitcher lifts her left leg knee high,
slightly twists her shoulders and throws the ball.
It flies fiercely through the winds.
CLINK! The batter hits the ball.
A lighting strike to first base.

First base: there goes my face, the flying ball.
Her arm the bat, her hand the tip.
My head boomerangs off the wall
and a trail of tears die down my shivering shirt.
I fail to answer the questions out of a primitive need
to escape her disciplines.
Her love came with the conditions of slaps
and bruised chins from being pushed off porches.

The next batter approaches the square
with dust rising behind her.
The pitcher flings the softball. A fireball forms
from fast motion.
The confident batter claims the ball
and sends it through the skies on the sidelines.
       She hits me again unexpectedly; foul play.
       Humiliation rings throughout the room.
Another chance is given to the batter.
She makes her mark and shoots for first base.

The Magick of Healing

The former for second.

Second base: I'm left worthless
still standing and conquering my fears of failing
and falling into the hardness of the floor.
Why not just talk without striking?
Is softness and compassion a fool's way
to resolution and peace?
I guzzle down the confusion
while searching for answers I can't conjure.
I'm soaked and covered with an anxious cloak
pleading for the madness to cease. My eyes tell it all.

The last batter smiles at the pitcher. —*She knows.*
Hey, batter batter! The crowd chants eager for a win or strike.
        Fear floods my guts and chest. I hear its footsteps.
The pitcher smirks in return shooting a curve ball.
The batter sends the ball flying over the field
beyond the diamond
beyond the trees, the skies, the cosmos.
Home run!

Home run: she hits me a final time.
I fall back into the floor disappointed
scared, frightened and confused.
Middle school was a terribly horrific
moment in my existence.
I wanted death from being accused
of carrying in eight grade.
I'd trade this life for a slither of a break at any moment.

The team celebrates their win.
The teams stand opposite of each other in parallel lines.
They slowly walk in opposite directions.
Their arms extend out and form a chain
of ongoing high fives and they eventually shake hands.
—*Good game.*

We bond over my tragedy.
I jape and joke about being hit against the wall
to cope with the fear, humiliation, anger of being a runt.
A recessive gene. Submissive.
I sacrifice my dignity for a celebration,
a moment to regain my humanity
that was slapped away forcefully to find
answers to questions I still can't quite recall.

We laughed, trauma bonding. Me being the fool.
What a shameful victory and sweet defeat.
Game over.

How often do we explore
the shadows of our parents?
It is not always apparent
that they too once suffered.
They snuffed out their firepits
with their own punctured palms.
They skinned themselves until
the white meat showed
to keep us warmed and clothed.
This is no excuse for whatever abuse
we may have experienced.
Are we willing to explore these shadows?

They Can't Hear Past My Skin

Twelve-foot beings of colorful hues
stomp and roam the planet
I am one of them, yet
I often wonder
What can I offer?
Their radiance and brilliance inspire me
We explore vast seas in space
and write symphonies that reveal
the never-ending rhythm of cosmic creation

I have many talents to share
Thoughts to contribute for a greater globe
When I greet those beings with openness
judgement and disgust spit on me
I must pay in pulchritude
and be otherworldly
as long as I remain familiar
and emulate what is popular
I must be a clone
with my original buried and decayed

They say, *please be unique and different,*
but not like that
Your uniqueness must fit
between these lines
You are measured on a scale of one to ten
Imagine,
they oblige themselves to create your identity
based on a number

Numbers are the language of God
that reveal the truth of our simulation
Why then, are the value of my gifts
determined by the height of my cheek bones
by the glass of my skin
the slim of my waist
or the silk of my hair?
Why then, is my worth seen
by the light of my knees?
How can you measure me
on a number line
when beauty is rooted
in the imagination of the mind?
When the mind exists
outside the presence of a body?

I want to help humanity
co-create a place for us to thrive
I guess I'll have to wait until
I tone the muscle in my thighs
Until my pants size is less than nine
How sublime
their ears go deaf
and they lose respect
because they believe
that my skin does not shine

KaSandra Turner

Healing seems so distant
barely visible through a telescope
Even when a way is made for me
I just can't seem to go

I think I'll stay here another fall
to watch the leaves on the trees
shed and shimmer
to brown, burgundy, and yellow
and meet the ground
while longing for you

It's Always Those

It's always those
who seem to have the answers
who seem to see with reason
and higher wisdom
that are reserved for just that
Have we no place for love and kinship?

It's always those
who offer their spines
as steppingstones and ladders
for others to reach for the moon
Whose tears form fountains
for others to drink of
Have we no place for healing?

It's always those who are kind
compassionate and gentle
who are overlooked and only seen
when it benefits another
All for those others
to scurry back to the very ones
who pushed them deep in dirt

It's always those
who love without condition
who are taken for granted
and are only missed
when they are gone.

You stare into their soul
and sense a sacred beauty
worth slaying demons for.
You'd pull the sun himself
down and destroy his core
if it meant you'd see
their smirk or smile
because they're all the light
you need.

You offer your tears as tribute
to ensure their cleansing.
You slice yourself
into fractured fragments
to guide them to wholeness.
And even when you've signed
your name in blood and ink
and sold your soul
in exchange for their freedom,
they'll still make love
to someone else less worthy.

-Collateral damage

I'm drifting in a void
and I just can't seem
to find a way back
to reality
Nothing exists, but my screams
bouncing into nothingness
It's just me in the dark
yearning for a beam of light
to save me
No one hears me
and no one's coming

You'd think I was cursed
if I shared all my misfortune
You'd swear that a coven betrayed me
Sent their familiars
to claw and climb up my house
for wanting out the circle
Their breath breaking through my windows
and their werewolf bodies
plunging into my nightmares
claws first

In fact I have no coven
Just a book of shadows
full of coffee aged pages painted with my tears
My fears written in red ink
and power spells to summon healing
to stop the bleeding

Is it Better Up There?

We laughed in the heat of night
awake past the witching hour
We loved through our painful fights
Yeah, it was hate that we devoured
Our souls danced and intertwined
in the passion of our fires
I was better when I called you mine
cause it's you that I admire

Is it better up there where you are?
Baby, is it better up there where you are?
Is it better up there where you are?
Oh, is it better up there where you are?

I fought so hard for you to stay
Even gave you my own breath
It wasn't enough for you to say
you'd defeat the duel with death
I see your face through memories
They keep me up at night
They've turned into my enemies
I'm afraid I've lost the fight

Is it better up there where you are?
Tell me, is it better up there where you are?
Is it better up there where you are,
Oh love, is it better up there where you are?

Tell me there's a space for me

up there by your side
Tell me you'll come flying down
when it's my turn to die
I can't take living in this place
without you here with me
I'd rather be casted down to hell
than exist in this reality

Is it better up there where you are, my love
Is it better up there where you are?
Is it better up there where you are, baby
Is it better up there where you are

Is it better up there
is it better up there...
is it better up there where you are?

The Magick of Healing

I go hell when I go silent
Whispers of a plagued past
haunt my cries and pleas of pardon
I can't exist in a world
that chops me down
like trees cleared for a concrete jungle
I can't be still in my own mind
cause it's filled with their stories
and the chem trails of their wounds
sprayed purposefully for my demise
There are moments my mind wonders into
the space of their hateful charm
I find myself encapsulated
in a shell of thoughts that aren't mine

I contemplate deletion of my life sometimes
I discover myself
cascaded with the sins and afflictions
of a time
where I could have loved more gently
I loved as hard as I could
Perhaps that was the problem
I was wired to go hard
I rejected the power of softness
Rigid is my bleeding heart
as it yearns for that softness
to breathe and be free
of those chemtrails and thoughts
I'm stuck in this entangled
everlasting loop
of descending into the captivity

of my afflictions
until freedom becomes me again

You wanted my core
So, you drilled into my rib cage
like a hammer drill to concrete
when all you had to do
was ask.

KaSandra Turner

I sometimes hear the night
tiptoe through my window
It's usually during a new moon
when the clouds hide
under the dress of darkness

I hear all the words I don't say
see the poems I don't write
on display
I'm dismantled
My heart drags against my chest
aching for relief
I'm stuck in the belief
that things just won't change

The Magick of Healing

The shadows reach to hold me
The silence is louder than my screeches,
It follows
I trip away afraid of being consumed
chewed, swallowed and spit out
Then again
it would be the warmest touch
I've felt since January
It sees through me
It the sun and me its moon

Why does this dense darkness
tall as oaks
have a pulsing beat
and persistently visits my corner?
I see *hands* void of shape and color
slither on my cream blankets at noon
I don't sense danger,
but escapism is how I cope
It whispers my name each night
and lowly growls, *I see you*
The daunting darkness hugs me numb
until it drags me into the further

57

My bones laughed one day,
You hit like you're scared of pain.
Break us all the way.

I'd rather hurt me
and drag myself straight to hell
to burn in my flames.

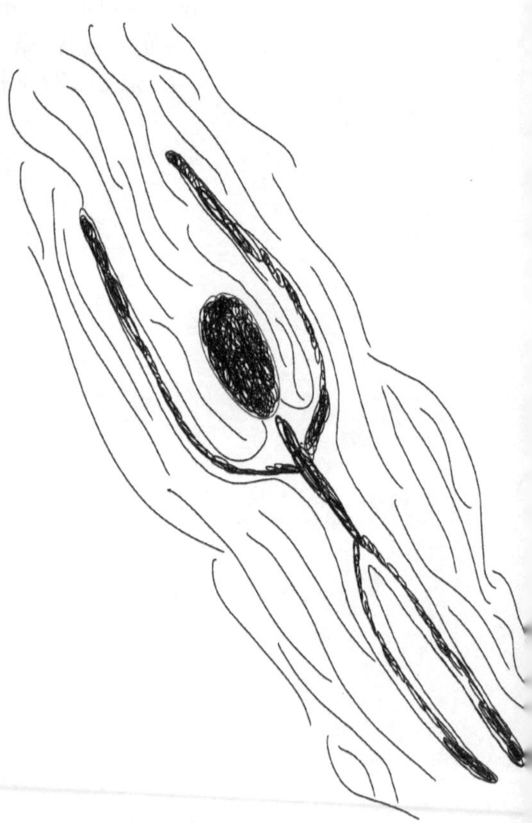

How ironic,
I have to halt my healing
to navigate your psyche
and help you figure out
why you keep hurting me.
The cloth and bandage I made for me
to clean and cover my wounds
I use for you instead.

Have We No Honor?

Clouds gray and rumbling
I sense the start of a storm
brewed by the broken heart of God
She supplies us with her endless green
nurtures with her fallen fruit
and homes us with her trees

I'd say we ought to unite
to keep her balanced and thriving,
but we fail to keep her clean
We claw each other without shame
before we hold ourselves first
We are programmed
to see our brothers and sisters
as enemies

Oh, Great Earth Mother!
Her lands are plagued with debris
Toddlers with no training we are
only our mothers taught us
to praise and honor God

Is not God the one who gives all?
The one who will supply all our needs
should we only ask to receive?
How dare we treat machines
like cousins
sisters
brothers

and friends
yet spit on the Earth
as if she is a foe

62

A ditch well covered
guides me to its bottom pits.
I'm stuck in the earth.

KaSandra Turner

I Wish I Knew When

No one and nothing prepares you
for the rage you feel
when your forever person passes
No one warns you
that you'd be entangled and webbed
in emotions and feelings
that belong to you and everyone else

No one hints at the fact
that you may be blamed
for your partner's death
as if you have the say so
of when their time comes
or the how
or the why it happened
as if you can prevent a fate
awarded to us all
As if you didn't try to keep them alive
As if you didn't breathe your breath
into their body
when they were already gone

No one told me
I'd be widowed at twenty-eight
grieving while three months postpartum
with two babies to raise
How do I live the rest of my life
when I have so much left to do
and so far to go alone?

The Magick of Healing

I am never proud when a loved one passes on
I will never not care for their homegoing
I feel ashamed to say
that I feel a bit of gay
to see family and old friends
together again

It takes a sad day to unite our tears
despite sleeping in sperate rooms
Distance becomes the noise
a carried tune
we all sing to
until a tragedy strikes

-So, when's the next funeral?

KaSandra Turner

I sometimes secretly stare up
while the ceiling sucks my eyes into its raft
I ache to see faces I never will
I get rejected by the world at first glance
and tribes of people I know I belong to
They won't accept people like me
Closed practices are kept secret
from mislabeled entities
I'm a part of this land
but they won't welcome me
A sad story of my ancestry
I wish I had mothers to teach me
the original rituals and ceremonies
of my indigenous family
I'm torn wishing I could understand
how I don't belong
to a place on the planet I was born on
This earth is abundant with wisdom in its dirt
They hide it in plain sight
in laws
paintings
treaties
and sacred texts
Yet, I'm made to believe
that these truths are not made
for my eyes to see
They will judge before offering to teach
the truth they tuck between their legs
I wish my elders were here to pray for me

Accepting that you are suffering from trauma is sometimes just as rigorous as going through the healing process. Accepting the reality of your trauma really does have a way of eating a hole through your chest. It feels like being thrown into a sea of blades and upward facing swords when we realize that we have been wounded and weakened. We sometimes become numb to the feeling of our environment. Nothing makes sense. We find ourselves trapped in a labyrinth formed by our own confusion and inner conflict.

Which way leads to clarity? Which was is a path to peace? How do we set ourselves free?

I'm Just Here to Heal

I work my magick in the name of good
Every herb, flower, resin, and incense
is birthed by the Great Mother
is blessed and charged under the stars and moon
for my highest intention
I am here to serve others through the Divine
I need no blood of yours or theirs
to work my magick or fuel my craft
Yet, when you hear that I am a Witch
you hiss and damn me to eternal suffering
Fear awakens and taints your perception of me
as if your faith does not stem from the old ways

My grandmothers conjured healing
from the waters of their wombs
They spun beauty from their burns and wounds
My ancestors,
whom you honor and worship in secret
whose prayers you chant under your tongue
smoothed and paved paths with their bare hands
that lead me to divinity
Unafraid,
they casted spells in the name of *the almighty*

You're blinded by hatred when I show up ready
to offer healing in my authenticity
Before I am a witch, I am a woman
a nonbinary soul expressed in feminine form
having a human experience

to thrive and be my best
Like the food you eat that you don't grow
the hate you give is not yours
You see the worst in me,
but all I can see
is the fact that you need healing

They say you can feel the heart
skip a beat before it breaks
I'd lend a limb to live it
My molars could be extracted
while I'm wide awake
The dentist blankly staring through my throat
I'd still wonder and wait for the pain
A bomb could, BOOM!
in the middle of my chest
I could be sliced in half
cut clean with a chainsaw
from my head down to my privates
I'd wear confusion across my parted face
wondering why it doesn't hurt

I'd drain the blood from me
as an offering
in exchange of being slammed
as long as I could feel
something
someone
anything
Let me know I'm living
Anything is better than nothingness

How much suffering will us humans endure before we tap into our power and will to rise above our suffering? How much blood and resources must be shed and lost before we decide unite and create a sustainable and healthy world? Why is it that at the moment we are faced with survival or our demise, we have this instinct to stretch beyond our limitations? Suddenly everything we took for granted becomes the very things that push us to live another moment. We pull thoughts and strength from places we've never reached or discovered when red laser lights are pointed directly at the center points of our foreheads.

It is at the point of survival that the horrors we keep hidden within our shadows are revealed. What we are capable of is suddenly the highlight that exposes our light, shadows or balance of both. Are survival and death the only incentives that inspire our need to reach beyond our might? Are they truly what keep us locked away from our ability to unite and love? Does death and survival erase our ability to be rational and intelligent enough to know that we are not enemies, but a multiplicity of singularities here experiencing this dream world simultaneously and together? Does pain and our thirst for revenge and superiority simmer and smother our ability to be compassionate?

We have allowed ourselves to become so desensitized and disconnected from ourselves and each other that our sense of humanity and compassion are overridden. For the need to make it out alive. To be the one. But, what is life without love or connection? What is living without the illusion of death? What is love without compassion?

We so are pumped and plagued with horrors and atrocities that emerge from our screens that the human experience has somehow become centered around spiritual, emotional, and mental cannibalism. We will drink our own blood for the last hit of fear as if fear is the only route to evolution. We have such a capacity for greatness as individuals as a cosmic clan that those who we have given our power away to strategically prey on our ignorance for the sake of control. They consume our essence and submit to energies that exist beyond our comprehension. People trade self awareness for a fix of fame and monetary gain. Individuals will trade their honor, gifts, talents and their ability to contribute to world unity for fulfilling their desires despite the perpetuation of chaos and destruction it encourages. Separation has been branded onto our brains and our first reaction is to defend as if there is something or someone out there that threatens our existence. If there was, wouldn't the wise thing be to unite?

We are mightier when are tapped into our own individual power and collective strength. Isn't it more difficult to break several sticks and branches at once than it is a singular one? Imagine if we decided that surviving wasn't enough. Imagine if we allowed ourselves to evolve past needless selfishness and destruction. How much greater would the world be?

I agree that nature and who we are is quite chaotic. But, this does not confiscate our ability to transcend beyond the chaos. We must do better if we are to thrive as a species. There is more to life than fear and separation. There is love, peace and freedom should we choose to unite.

The Magick of Healing

I replayed the scenes where they called me ugly
as if they could see my insides
as if they didn't see the endless love
and unconditional understanding I gave
They used to call me ugly
because my features just didn't sit right
I didn't fit a mold that mirrored
their programmed beliefs
of how a woman should appear

And then there were those
who were in love with my features
because I emulate the rawness of Earth
My deep brown skin blends seamlessly with her clay
Pages of wisdom and love
are written in my wrinkles
Flowers and trees grow from my scalp
My coils extend beyond the cosmos
The creator herself flows through my blood
They appreciated my unaccepted features
and saw a soul through my eyes
But because I faithfully meditated
on the chaotic perceptions of others
my beauty rituals failed and it showed

I don't understand the human condition
of accepting others based on their genetics
They stare at me and see a distasteful body
while I peer through them and see a sacred soul

If I lit a candle for each time

I was called ugly or unattractive
picked on by children and adults
picked out and discarded like dark purple jelly beans
I'd light up the state of New York
and it would remain bright for a lifetime

The Magick of Healing

I grabbed a thorned rose
with eager hands and desperate fingers
I ached to marvel in its beauty
in my own sacred space
A stream of salt water surprisingly
escaped down my cheeks
as my thumb tip throbbed and leaked
I stared at this white rose
wondering why the tear raced eagerly
for freedom from my ducts
I was careful not to disturb her petals
I was engulfed in the confidence
that I'd carry her pulchritude
in glass to sit before my window
to revive me from the death of dullness
I'd provide her replenishment from solar beams
How dare she not know of this!
Regret and foolishness filled my clayed vessel
Entitlement, selfishness, and boldness noosed my neck
How dare she protect her energy
while hurting me in the process

KaSandra Turner

I'd rather pace a path of freedom
than die on the pitchforks of escapism
I'd prefer my chains be melted
by the breath of my will
to love and be loved

I'd prefer the comfort of a demon
whose tongue reeks of uncomfortable truths
Who will claw my insides and expose my light
as it leads me to enlightenment

I'd rather dwell in nurturing shadows
in the essence of the void
as my wounds warp to fractals
and merge with my cries
I'd rather meet my demise
and bask in the light of freedom

You Sound Like a White Girl

I didn't know that pronouncing every syllable
sounded like the color white
until after I learned to read and write
The kids in my classes in elementary
mocked me and amused themselves
with the comedy of my vocabulary
They blanketed their jealousy
with the comforters of their laughs
Their envy and ignorance dug pits
in the soils of my self-esteem
I aced my tests and at times got B's
buzzing through my report cards
They seemed to devour me alive
because I strived to make my mother proud
Because the words on my pages danced in harmony
They were proof that I could see beyond the news
and reach beyond the cages of the Jordan Downs projects
that were projects for copper-colored Kings and Queens
We were marginalized with margins
that measured wider than the bunk beds
stacked like Lego blocks in our small bedroom
filled with pinks and blues
It was words that I painted on paper
to escape the earthquakes and raptures
of my bullies and oppressors at school and home

They broke the concrete of my mind
I was scared dead before I shrugged off to school
Teachers starved to see what would seep from my head

KaSandra Turner

They had stickers waiting at their desks
because I gave nothing less than my best
The kids would separate themselves from me
like oranges, yellows, blues and greens
But how did they know what white sounded like
when our school couldn't even afford organic food?
As if literature was reserved for those with white skin
My intelligence ended where their perceptions would begin
They identified me as an Oreo
But they didn't know,
that it wasn't the white middle that watered my mouth
It was the flavor and sound of that chocolate cookie crumbling
and cascading over my palate that lured me in for more

I was teased for winning perfect attendance awards
because having brown skin meant my destiny was sealed
I was expected not to surpass the height of their heels
My wooden school desk was supposed to be
my home away from fear
Yet school was a parallel reality where my dreams were nightmares
I used to tell myself, *the words are out there*
You just have to find them
So, I searched the jungles deep within my kinky curls
I found the best words that made my writing
brilliant enough to be displayed behind tall, shiny glass
that reflected their disappointments in fourth grade
I hardly had anyone to play with
because I could barely speak with Ebonics
Because I didn't look like Cinderella
with the shiny blue dress
or Belle with the pretty voice and brown hair

77

The Magick of Healing

I forced myself to codeswitch
like witches warping into muggles in daylight

I was teased for the very thing I was passionate about
Learning beyond my limits
Yet somehow this was normal for those
who were thin with blonde and brown hair
who had pretty pink lips lined with lipstick at age six
Whose parents drove Bentleys
and went out with their families
for breakfast before the school bell rang
My breakfast sometimes consisted of an ass whooping
and a, "TAKE YOUR ASS TO SCHOOL!"
Once they inserted *bitch* for my name

I was the anomaly for reading as good as my teachers
I ate more words in a minute
than they'd get paid in a paycheck
I wasn't hood enough to be tribal
And we all see that my skin isn't snow
So, in what world was I safe in?
I wasn't light enough to hang with kids with light skin
Not perfectly pretty enough
to play with my peers at the jungle gym
I was the odd ball bouncing itself with no hands

I speak beside my ancestors when I say
that words are the way for me
Words are not reserved for the privileged
over the poor when we pour our love over our poems
our books

our essays and journals too

One day you'll need a telescope to find me
because I'll be levitating higher than apostrophes
writing my personal book of life for the world to see
One day the world will see that I am destined to be
someone who surrendered to their calling
to help promote world unity
To offer gifts to the great masses of humanity
I won't dress my kinks in silk pressed hair
just to emulate Emily
And if you see me in a weave,
just know I'm growing my hair underneath
to prevent the damage of heat
And yes, it can grow beyond the limit of your life line

I'm proud of EVERY version of me
And I look. Fucking. GOOD.

When you hear me speaking eloquently
just know I'm self-taught
and do NOT tell me
that I sound like a white girl

Period.

They say that mirrors reveal our true selves
through our reflections
That they are portals to our internal world
That you are what you see

I stared into my mirror
searching for signs of beauty
It cracked and bled
That's better
Now I look more like you, it said

I lay still and shift through memories
I'm worn and withered
from life's lessons
My emotional bones
are barely healed from breaking
Stones are half dissolved in my stomach
Saturn has been cruel to me
I finally surrender

The Magick of Healing

There comes a point in our lives
when we're healing, you know?
That we just get tired of being tired
sick of feeling sick
and done with being done.
We get tired of walking into
the same walls in the same maze
feeling lost in loops of hopelessness
and misery.

We get tired of laying
our emotional bodies over
the tears of those we love most
and others all to feel
depleted, drained, and damaged in the end.
Something has to give.
Something has to change.
I have given my power away
for far too long.

It showed 12:34am on the clock
as a sizzling, simmering knot in my gut
forced me awake
Electricity ran through my hands
My third eye tingled

My intuition lifted me out of bed
I headed straight into my apothecary
and kneeled at my altar
A guide whispered,
It's time

84

Let the rituals begin.

Rituals

"Ritual is the continuous act of dedicating oneself to fulfilling a desire. It is what keeps *any* individual devoted, disciplined, and aligned throughout their journey of healing, manifestation, and self-mastery."

-KaSandra Turner

I tried to find my way home
I found myself in a misty night
My feet feverously ached
from the unforgiving cold
that carried me to stillness

One step...
two steps...
three steps...
THUD!

I dropped into a lucid dream
A demon dragged me through a doorway
Another doorway led to a maze
that led to trapped doors
and more doors led to deadened paths
The only way out was to awaken
To return to my numbed body

Ironic it was
to return to something
I could no longer feel
The demon with nine-inch claws
thirteen feet tall
stood and stared
Wake up
it growled
You've got work to do...

The Magick of Healing

My screams have grown quiet
My lungs fail to bleed out the depths
I don't shine
My mind is plagued
with all the tears I leave behind
Opaqued dreams of deception
leave me no space for revelations
I'm trapped in a sunken space
submerged in the sparkles of my fears

Divine, reveal to me
that which I can't see
Or am I just subconsciously refusing
to share eyes with the truth
that will set me free
and raise me from this drunken dream?

KaSandra Turner

Enough is Enough

I grew weakened by the pressures of self-hate
Afflictions and sins often invaded my peace within
I grew angry and full of vengeful rage
when I shattered my confidence
with the bats of their ideologies
abuse and ignorance
I lost myself in their whirlwinds
of dysfunction and self-destruction
I grew tired of piecing back together
the millions and billions of infinitesimal pieces
I allowed them to shatter
They injected me with their turmoil
and tainted the purity
that kept me within close proximity
of my higher being

I grew numbed and knew that my time had come
to reclaim the power that was drained from me
when he watched me bathe
and touched the innocent parts of me
His hardened flesh still lingers in my mouth
The chocolate he used to paint
the insides of my cheeks with his meat
still leaves my tongue bitter
pleading for remedy
I still see the darkness that knee high sock
blanketed over my five-year-old eyes
I showered in scorching water
desperately clawing and peeling off the filth

the world bled on my skin
I stuck my hand down my throat
and grabbed my heart from my abyss within
I squeezed tighter
and tighter
and tighter
until the hate formed tar within my tear ducts
and oozed out from my eyes
I strangled the little love I had left for myself out
I swallowed the swords
of their unconditional loathing for me
Each spell they casted
were sharpened claws that scratched
the lining of my throat
They left me aching and weak
scavenging for a final death

Stained with my own tarred tears
I pleaded with angels and demons
I bent and begged at their waist and knees
searching for God in hopes that she'd hear me
I gave my final howl of grief
with all the breath that was left of me

When my body was bruised and broken
a word was spoken
A raging divine feminine energy
that was so sweet and gentle
yet intense and geared for war
ready to strangle and destroy
covered my nearly dead body

KaSandra Turner

Bring them to me, she said,
I'll trample on their heads

Free Us, Great Mother

Divine mother, Kali
who protects her children with unforgiving might,
lurid waves of blood and bodies
spill over lands where lambs cry.
The Earth roars and rumbles furiously.
Your brilliant beasts and children mourn
for a time of night to decay the day
where crumbled buildings claimed the grounds.
Cloak us in your raging love.
We honor your karmic dances of death.
Defeat them, Great goddess.
We beseech your protection from their savagery.
They have reigned a heinous terror
and imbalanced the flows of universal rhythm.

Let the balance of dark and day
be the emblem of your power.
Let your shadows of darkness
shower over this plane.
For there is no light seen
without the void of black that shines.
Your grace is the shelter that keeps us safe
away from the dread of those
that conquer ruthlessly.
May your darkness be the light
that brings life to barren things.
Restore our faith in grace and love
through streams of hate to reclaim this place.
Charm and charge our blood

so that we may be whole once more.

Exalted Mother Kali,
your power is great.
Your destruction is necessary
to demolish the disorder.
Please give rise
to the destructive waves
of your divinely feminine rage.
May your vengeance restore
peace in this space.

Return to Sender

I wrote their names on craft brown paper
in black, permanent ink
Their projected wounds and ten years of my tears
bled into that letter
I told the Divine to return their energy
to make the image of me
sting and burn their eyes so harshly
that they'd gouge them out
with their own infected nails
Let all that they inflicted be on display
Make them rot in their flames

Their wickedness I summoned
to be returned ten-fold
I burned that petition down to blackened ash
I buried the ashes as an offering to Earth Mother
I gave her my tears and reclaimed my worth
I chose to cut connections of hate
sadness, and pity
One by one
I watched them suffer
They tried to return and apologize,
but pain was served
and justice was mine.

Let us all meditate
simultaneously
Dance naked, titties out
Hair up and let down
Moon shining against softened skins
Intentions set for the collapsing
of the patriarchal system
outdated with dreams of greed

Let us throw our asses
in circles in the circles we casted
to the musical crumbling
of their falling empire

We will reclaim the world
to bring back balance
and honor our bare bodies
Make them grovel and kiss our feet
and dwell in the chaos
they brought upon this world

The Magick of Healing

You tease me for not looking like you
You come into my world
to mock and make a fool of me
How about I skin your scalp
to make a wig of your hair
sew it to a doll and gift it to your mother
Would that suffice?
Maybe I should skin you alive
and wear you as a coat
to protect me from the cold of your judgments
Your blood painting my face and body
Or wear your arms as sleeves
your eyes as contacts
your stomach as a bag
How about I take your teeth
and turn them into jewelry
Then again, they wouldn't sell much
Perhaps I should just cut out your tongue
tie it in red string
and pin it to a plate
Place a red candle in the middle
to shut you up
What will it take
for you to shut your mouth?
What will it take
for you to leave me alone?

KaSandra Turner

Bladed Boomerang

Where is the beginning of inflicting pain?
It might be in the hands of the righteous
who have seen God without the need of binoculars
With eyes that rape open heaven's fences
and bladed tongues tipped with mischief,
smeared in the blood of butterflies

Does it ever circle back to its center point?
Is there a force whom dare divines
a feasible reason for the return of stones thrown
at the backs of the beheaded?
My mental melts from fires of spiteful sparks,
heart stops and is ripped away from graceful places
My screams are used as feed for the lustful with unholy dreams
of consuming minds in marred bodies pumped with fear
unkempt and unclean

I dare to dream of a life where I wash away the absence
of their respect, and declare my self-love to come storming back
into my arms stretched from wrapping my body
to protect my soul from being sucked through straws
that lead to hollowed chests aching for a mother's touch

Karma takes her sweet time; she's unfaithful and unkind
I refuse to wait for her to deliver me from petrifying evil
I'll smite those who wronged me; unlucky, hateful bitches
Unfortunately for them
the ones they beat and bullied became the witches

97

Purge and Banish

It was the witching hour on a Saturday night
when the winds whirled and howled
I heard the screeches of my traumas
bang against my shredded chest
Chaos carelessly consumed my crying insides
and consistently clawed its nails in my back
and left blistering burns and scars
The wounded world's words of poison
plagued and pierced my passions
and when I ached for death
they stabbed me instead

There was a roar rumbling in my womb that night
that left me dizzy with sickness
Acid boiled in my stomach
I was pregnant with my own afflictions
and swollen from societal pressures
to be what they idealized
I was expected to take the form of their lies
and limited imaginations
I wanted connection
So, I stretched my skin and molded my mind
desperately begging to be believed and seen
I lost myself in their lucid dreams
I knew that to find myself,
I had to purge and release

That night when the clock
read twelve past twelve

KaSandra Turner

I showered in warm water
I chanted prayers to cleanse my aura
I drew a bath with brewed herbs and roots
Epsom salt, dead sea salt,
and charcoal powder
Burdock root to purge and dispel
spells spoken and planted into my psyche
Chicory root to slice and break
the buildup of calamity
Dragon's blood to intensify me
and send my enemies fleeing
Frankincense to exorcise
the oppressors who shapeshifted
into demons and formed fragments and lies

After soaking and chanting for thirty-three minutes
I fully rinsed and dried myself
I dressed in all black strapped lingerie
and a midnight silk hooded robe
I invoked the spirits of sage and holy wood
I casted a circle with black salt and chalk
and sealed it with a protection spell
I sang and summoned the waters of the west
Danced to attract the fires of the south
Called out to the whispering winds of the east
I offered my vessel to the earth up north
Conjured the source of spirit within me
and declared that I have purged
and purified myself clean!

I refuse to hold and harness

the filth of those who hardly know
what their palms look like
I found my release through magick
and they met a mental demise

A Protection Sigil

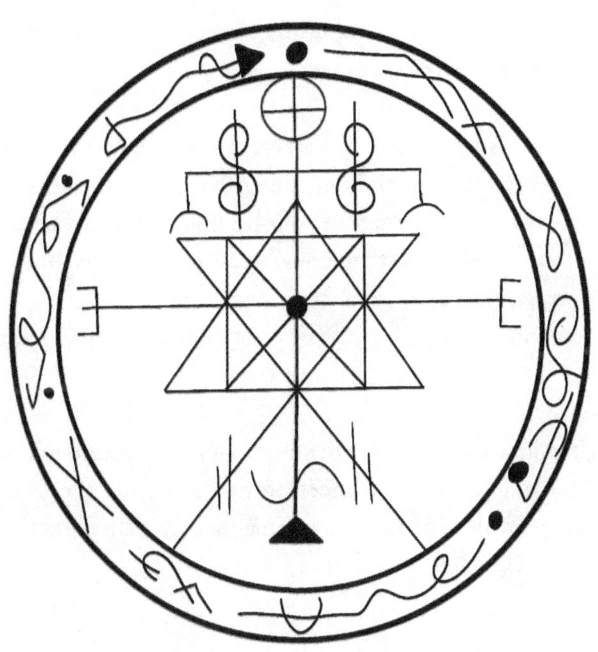

Intuitive Message Revealed

Sometimes purging sounds like screams scratching and torturing the walls. It looks like heavy breathing and sweating. Regurgitating your insides literally and figuratively. It can appear as rocking back and forth. Not wanting to consume anything except water. Pushing everyone away to be in your own space. Angrily cutting your hair out. Ripping the weave out while your tears smear your mascara and eyeliner forming a trail of thick black rivers down your face. Purging sometimes looks like not wanting to talk for extended periods of time. Like not showing up at gatherings to keep your energy away from the people you love.

Purging is a process of healing. Whatever it looks like for you, honor it. Be present with yourself and remember that your journey is unique. This is a necessary stage in your healing journey. When you empty yourself out and reject what you've always believed about yourself, you can then replace the toxins with the nourishment of your authenticity. Purging is a part of your spiritual reset where you send all the things that are not of your essence fleeing.

Your spirit guides are gently, yet firmly encouraging you to release the resistance to purging. Your ancestors and guides are always there for comfort and clarity. Humbly welcome their guidance and they will lead you back to love.

-Time stamp: October 21, 2023, 4:44pm EST

I lit a white candle for you on Moon Day
I wore white and wrapped my hair
in a pink velvet headwrap
I cleansed my feet in rose water
I thought that maybe
Just maybe, baby
that you'd come home
if I softened and smelled
like sweet pink roses
and honeysuckle
I laid lavender and jasmine petals
on the ground in hopes that
they would lead you back to me
Here I am
with my sacredness sucked away
my white robe stained with my tears
weeping and waiting for you

A Spell for Self-Love

Place a rose quartz crystal on a cleansed altar space
and the best picture of you in a decorated frame
Your favorite flowers grown with respect to Earth Mother
May the love you have for her be for you just the same
Place a glass of spring water free of filth and impurities
on the altar to erase the dirt and muck of insecurities
A light pink candle caressed and anointed with jasmine oil
May the hate and disdain of any enemies be foiled
Gently massage the oil into the marks on your skin
Let it seep into the unseen darkest depths within
With an unguarded heart honest with tears, if you must
light the candle and gaze upon its flame with trust
Project your voice boldly and say
this spell out loud as many times as you may,

I release the self-hate I formed from fear
I cleanse myself with my own holy tears
I leave my pain below the strength of my knees
I declare that my love is returned to me
I welcome the love I poured out back in
I walk in the light of my beauty within
I am rich and abundant with wealth and self-worth
I wisely choose to honor and put myself first
I speak of and to myself in the highest degree
I declare in the name of God that I am free!
May all ill will be returned times three
This spell is cast,
so shall it be!

Your Glamour Magick Sucks

I wonder if they really think
that if they *charm* enough makeup brushes
smile long enough to form a hammock on their face
and *speak* with glittery vocabulary foreign to our elders
that those who have cried lakes to their feet
will not hear the truth hidden behind their teeth
I wonder if they think
that if they *wear* crystal necklaces long enough
their beads reaching their soles
we will be oblivious
to their poverty and lack of knowledge
or the shadow work they omit
because cheap beats the long road to luxury
that we are oblivious to the demons
who wear white on their right shoulders
and call out to us for freedom

Don't look through me, my glass will crack
Just focus on the shiny crystals that match my nails and teeth
Focus on the turbans that cover my scars from arogance
Look! -I've grown a long beard
I wear white flowing pants drenched in animal sacrifice
That makes me qualified to tell you
that I'm more spiritual than you
Besides, I've got bad ass tattoos
and can read tarot on a surface level
I can do a love reading for you
to keep you crying back
to escare the human condition

of longing love and light

They hide behind posts
long enough to cloak them times three
Their words are rotten bread
covered with the sweet thickness of honey
They keep their egos in their workings
We do not hide behind lenses
with backgrounds of plastic plants we can't tend to
Our healing and magick
did not begin on screen
It started with us learning
to weave through the streets
Learning how to walk along the path of our tears
We built bridges from the crumbs
left behind by our families
to help bridge the gap between
worlds at war with one another
Our magick and beliefs were birthed
within the wombs that nurtured us
throughout our depression and anxiety attacks

Like fruit, flowers, and trees
we come colorful and abundant
with shapes that emulate waves and fractals
that warp forming reality
We are a community of spiritual bad asses
here to shake shit up
And although some of us love
engaging in various forms of divination
we don't need cards or crystal balls to read you

Some of us are self-taught
Others have had the honor
to drink from their elders' cups

Either way, we did and STILL do
the required work
So, instead of faking, you too can learn
how to work real magick.

Go read a fucking book.

We are not a trend or an aesthetic
or books you can burn
if we don't contain the pictures
of your beliefs.
We are not bracelets that make you look pretty
or spoons to feed your dirty mouths.
You wipe your noses with the love we share
when instead you should hold it
gently and press it against your chest.

Learn to admire the beauty of gardens
filled with borage and chamomile
without picking their petals
or taking them home to die.
Respect us witches and honor our craft
lest you wish to feel the wrath
of the Goddess.

Poets and Witches

A poet creatively expresses their experiences
and moves winds with words
We find the beauty and mystery
in places where others
have ripped their eyes out
We take what is left to rot and whither
and give it life by exploring its wonder
We *awe* at the invaluable and honor its form
We enhance the vibrancy of its essence
through imagery and exaggeration
New perceptions are birthed
through a poet's words

A witch will gather dried flowers and herbs
like catnip, rose, hibiscus and lavender
Place them in a pink candle
blessed with the smoke of sweetgrass
and anoint it with oil
infused with geranium
We will gaze upon a charmed mirror
with tunnel vision
staring beneath the skin
We'll chant spells
to find and enhance our beauty
and reveal it like shrubs
beneath blankets of snow
What I love most about poets and witches
is our power to move energy

with our minds and words
I appreciate us mostly because
of our ability to find the beauty in anything
We are relentlessly dedicated to our craft
and are marvelous weavers of life
How proud I am
to say that I am both

When we are unsure of ourselves
we often look for guidance
from the outside world
as if we only breathe out.

Does the air always pass us by?
Or does it also flow
around
above
below
and in us too?

-Go within

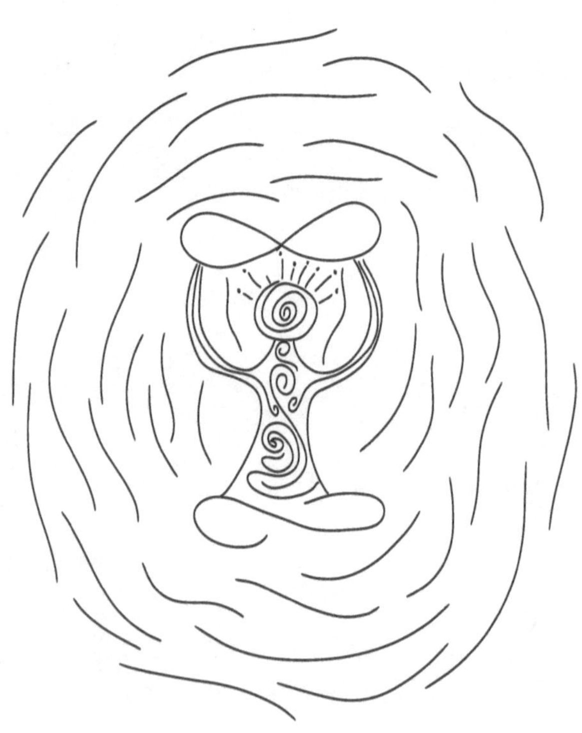

Third Eye Chakra

On a Monday night before bed, cleanse a purple candle with Florida water. Light the candle and speak these affirmations out loud:

I am divinely intuitive.
I am highly imaginative.
I trust my intuition.
I see the truth of intentions vividly.
I use my discernment when interacting with others.
I distinguish my intuition from my feelings and emotions.
I listen to and honor my inner compass.
I am connected to water and the energy of the moon.
I am open to the infinite possibilities of the universe.
I am psychic and embrace my supernatural abilities.
My visions are vivid and I interpret them clearly.
I surrender to the unknown because I am divinely led.
I differentiate my intuition from my imagination.
I am insightful and am connected to magick and mystery.
My third eye shows me the truth of this reality.

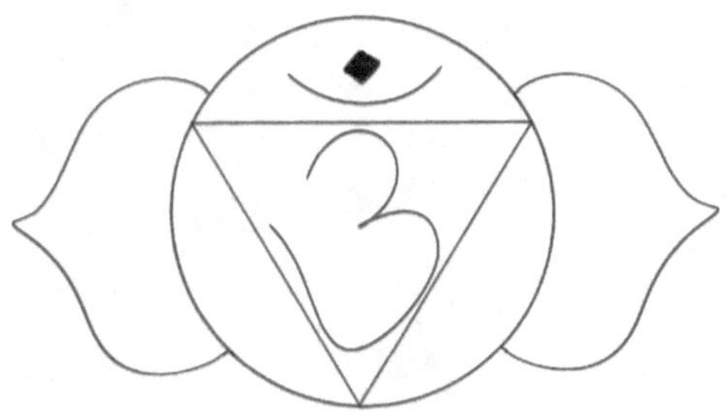

The Magick of Healing

My first home was among the stars
My second home was within my mother's womb
I spiraled down and forgot my essence
I started to experience people
I somehow, with the hate I learned
and confusion I consumed
strayed away and found my path blocked
with blocks and stones of illusions
Worldly situations seemed to constantly collide
and keep me anchored
from my greatest rewards and blessings
How will I ever find my way out
when I feel stuck and stagnant
within the spikes of my own mind?
I don't have the will to find the way
I have no choice but to surrender

To Open a Road

To my guides of love and light
whose strength is pure with will and might
Hear my call and humble plea
Unblock my path and guide my feet
I release all worry, doubt, and fear
This road be opened, my path be cleared
Reveal the road that welcomes me
This spell is cast,
so let it be!

A New Start

I place the soles of my feet on the heat of concrete
and let my toes dance their way to Earth
A magnetic pull shifts my frequency
and melts the mask I wear while lost in society
She pulses her beat through my feet, Earth Mother
and holds me in the womb of her nurture
Clouds cast away and make way for the stars to beam
A portal opens leading to my crown
Dark light is cast down from a new moon in Virgo
A new start, I see

Starlight never missed a pore on my cheek
I trust that this moment
is the start of a continued dream
Colors caress my internal void of infinite reflections
freeing me of black holes and pooled deceptions
I float and ponder in the dark
waiting for a sign,
a signal or spark
Visions of a higher version of me will manifest
and be uniquely expressed in my truest identity
A new start, I see

I'll take a palm sized portion of dried sweet basil
Nothing like the sweet scent of wealth through my nasals
Chamomile isn't just a seductress of sleep
Prosperity will flow daily in abundance right to me
Grapeseed, patchouli, and other oils to accompany
flowers and herbs to sit three days to eight weeks

I can feel it rumbling
A new start, I see

Source summons and sings to my soul through my purpose
Prayers and spells spoken and casted ignites the way
I revisit those moments I was stagnant and stayed
in the fear of my brightest future and losing those dear to me
But walking in alignment means devoting my energy
and following the node north of my magick and dreams
It seems the trees have turned their trunks towards me
as the stars light a pulsing pathway
A new start just for me

Ancestors

Your lineage lingers through my dancing feet,
    I will not betray you with dishonor.

Your favorite meals and snacks are placed upon the altar,
    I give to you in spirit as I have in flesh

I give thanks and gratitude in our conversations,
    I will not only call upon you when I am in need.

R&B oldies spark my speakers when I clean,
    your memories will forever live through me.

My children laugh at the memories where you checked me,
    they have grown to know respect.

Tobacco smoke is burned over my herbs,
    you showed me their spirits through intuitive visions.

Whiskey poured to the ground, cigar smoke fills the air,
    I will remember your birthday.

You passed elder hood down to me while in my early twenties.
You all have passed on and I will honor your memories.

Ancestor work is essential and nonnegotiable.
How else will I honor them?
How else will I study and discover their rituals?
How else will I unravel layers of myself?

How pathetic
that some will treat their ancestors
as they did in flesh.
Only connect with them in a time of need
when the money runs dry,
or when a loved one leaves.
A bond is only built
upon the condition of receiving.

I will always give to my ancestors
who gave to me in their former life.
Through food and songs.
Dancing, stories.
Genealogy.
To dishonor them
is to dishonor me.

Only calling on your ancestors when it benefits you is crazy work.

To Maintain Balance and Harmony

A student began to read a paragraph from a biology book. *An orgasm is a life form composed of complex...* The eighth-grade class laughed hysterically. I laughed to blend in and not expose the discomfort that swarmed me. I was grateful for having a darker complexion; my melanin saved me from the exposure of embarrassment by masking the heat in my cheeks.

How did we know about the result of sexual pleasure so early? How many of us were being taught these things at home and how did other kids learn? I learned what sex was before I had my first period. I was ashamed to be so advanced. I knew how and where to touch myself before I could release unfertilized eggs. I knew how to give head without having seen a penis at the age I was blindfolded. I would pray to God not to send me to hell because I could make myself orgasm without permission. I was taught how to properly wear a training bra by the man who touched me. How did he know how to wear it so well when he had no daughters or growing breasts himself?

Shame punished me for wanting to engage in sex when I became of age because my first experience was me performing orally with a sock around my head to the man I saw as my stepfather. I did not ask him to tell me where a penis was "supposed" to go, yet I knew not to tell. Even when one of my parents discovered that I told the truth when someone asked if he had molested me, their first reaction was to shame me and curse me out for not having told them *first*. No comfort was provided nor was there any justice given. I did not have access to a therapist, nor did I know how to obtain one at that time. These violations structured the foundation of my sexual relationships and is the reason for some of my kinks. I grew to inner-stand that instead of enjoying sex for spiritual connection and sexual pleasure I was operating from a space of sexual abuse and trauma.

I dove deep into my spiritual practice as a young adult and realized that sex, to me, is sacred. Minds use the body to evolve, experience pleasure, and explore each other whether it is done in solitude or with a partner(s). Sex can be used to manifest our desires into this reality by focusing our intention on the desire during the buildup of energy and release it out into the universe upon orgasm. We can engage in the process to transcend beyond our suffering and bodily limitations and expand our consciousness through a raw flow of energic exchange. It is through sexual exploration that we can unravel and integrate the rejected and newly discovered aspects of ourselves.

Sex is a language that can be expressed without words. We can express thoughts that we have trouble with communicating linguistically. Bodies bend, bond, and flow through unique rhythms that intertwine in harmony. When we harbor sexual trauma, we allow the disruption of energy to prohibit us from sexual expression, thus creating an experience of limitation, fear of intimacy and blocked creativity. Our unreleased traumas are the parasites that eat away at our ability to be bold and confident. We will sometimes attract others who validate our lack of self-confidence. This is why engaging in rituals and practices that help us release these stagnant energies is essential.

Working with the Sacral Chakra

On a Tuesday afternoon, cleanse an orange glass or pillar candle with Florida water. Light and recite these affirmations out loud:

I am safe to explore my sexuality.
I am safe and loved in my body.
I honor my body with divine love and care.
My sexuality reflects cosmic creation.
I give myself permission to experience sexual pleasure.
Creative energy flows through me freely.
I am a powerhouse of cosmic energy and divine inspiration.
The universe discovers itself through the fulfillment of my desires.
I am free of sexual trauma.
I honor my sexual orientation.
I communicate my sexual boundaries clearly.
I am bold, confident, and radiant.

You have every right to say no.

Anyone who makes you feel ashamed or criticizes you for wanting to wait is engaging in rape culture. No means no and any attempt afterwards is rape culture.

Sex does not have to be reserved for marriage if you don't want it to be.

Tell them if you are feeling any discomfort. It's okay to stop mid sex if you have a change of heart. You don't have to sit through it for the sake of another or out of fear of what they will say to or about you.

If you suspect that someone is aggressive and will harm you, do not engage. You don't need to follow logic. Your intuition will always lead you to the right reason.

You are not responsible for being sexually violated. What you wear, how you smell, or how you look is not an invitation for predatory behavior.

Your voice matters; I believe you.

KaSandra Turner

Spiritual Rape

You squat over that pot
like tomatoes hanging from an arched trellis
to dispel your menses into that spaghetti
The acid from the sauce and flavor of the meat mask
the smell and taste of your eggs
They did not bestow consent upon you
They are oblivious to your magick

You stroke yourself and save your seeds
to be squeezed into that Alfredo
so that the sight and consistency of your semen
marries the cream and color of that sauce
They did not gift you their consent
for you to work your magick to trance them
They are unaware of your treason

Enlighten me, beloved
How is this not spiritual rape?
You used your power to trance and trap them
against their knowledge, will and consent
They cannot explain how even though
they received no vibes or visions
and had not the smallest thought
or slightest intentions
of intertwining and combining their energy with yours
that they crave every inch of your slithering skin
That you stir feelings of lust, love and disdain
when you're near them
They feel deep within the cells of their blood

that there has been a violation of their spirit
They still cannot help but to nut
to the thought of you
They search for the first hit of betrayal
and become addicted
Your sacred fluids were drugs forced to the clean
and now they cannot dream
of a life without your rotting presence

Your hunger for praise and worship betrays you
Your traumas of abandonment and being overpowered
follow the stench and trail of your greed
You welcomed their demons and cannot understand
why the fruits of your labor have turned rotten

*May there be justice, balance, freedom and healing to those who have been
spiritually, mentally, emotionally and physically raped and assaulted.*

KaSandra Turner

Show Me Honor

If I bestowed the honor upon you
to gut me from the inside out
and lay my stomach on your table
you'll find the core of the sun
and it will scorch the wood to ash
If I allowed you
to spread me like curtains concealing
a room massed with mystery
your soul will ignite
and free you of that beastly body
My glittering oceans of pearls, gems and jewels
will spill over your bedsheets and pillows
Their shimmering shine
will glisten and summon your sins forth
You'll be anointed with the silk
smeared over my fingers
after my self-pleasure
Your spine will shiver
from the ripples of my moans
while your throat croaks with excitement
Your tongue will plead for salvation
from the atrocities of your malefactions
If you asked me to widen my mouth
you'll be pulled into a pulsing portal
leading to a pit
where seeds are swallowed
for abundance and life

You can find me twirling

The Magick of Healing

undressed in the night
with my curls lifting the skies
under a fierce moon filled with sunlight
Where the stars will fall under the command
of my twerking hips and electrical hands
I'll be belly dancing
to the heartbeat of the universe
until my knees are planted in the Earth
My kneeling knees will send frequencies
to the great Mother
Her moaning tunes will call out to me
My hands will be raised, as above
I'll be howling to sweep the clouds
and casting spells
to rain my blessings down, so below

When you come to me
expecting an experience
in laying with a witch
you'll be aghast and disquieted
by the slithering crawls of your corruptions
lest you have mastered your mind
and have embraced your divine feminine
Arrive respectful with your top lip sewn
to the bottom of your chin
Or your bottom lip stapled
to the tip of your nose
if you wish to immerse yourself
in the realms of my magick

I truly believe that for there to be magick
there must be a conscious observer.
The aware must project their will
into the universe as the doer.
It does not exist without intention.

Declaring black magick as evil
and white magick as good
is ignorantly dismissing
the intent and will of the practitioner.
We must leave out the racist undertones
from our workings
and slay it completely.

If the intention behind the working
is for self-gain, greed and to impede the path
of another at their detriment,
let us cast judgement
to protect one another.
May we honor our right to defend and protect.

Magick is neither black nor white.
It is the conscious mind that needs to be judged.

I Am

I am the driving force of your ferine desires
I am the heavens formed from the fires of hell
I am the Lillith who's freedom
is expressed through the vengeance of her will
I am the reason the stars fell
The reason fallen angels sing
You may think of me as a demon
Truly, I am an angel of night
who destroys the days glimmered in fallacies
to shower the wisdoms from things decayed
Between me, an abyss exists
that leads to portals beneath
the pressures of the seas
I am the mother of shadows, I set them free
My voice rings with a saturnine beat
I am the rejected and disdained, *the raunchy* who
explores her depths through restless sex The
forsaken yearns for my guidance and comfort I
am the color of obscurity
The one who births the freaks
that wreak true love in this realm
My darkness is light work
I encourage the world to embrace their wholeness
For what is light and liberation
without darkness and captivation?
To embrace my wrath
is to be worthy of a wisdom
that seeps through darkness and light
It is wise to worship me

as the weak have kissed your feet
It is an honor to exist in my presence
I am

Pussy Power

The pussy is a sacred space of healing
It has the gift of giving and receiving pleasure
It is the entrance to an internal void
A portal that welcomes spirits into this realm
It is valuable beyond human intelligence
Why else would predators feel the need
to prey upon and steal it
if it is not offered or given freely
or when requested?

You call us sluts when we embrace our pussy power
because it is proof that we have risen above
your primitive need to dominate and control
Even those of our kind will turn up their noses
if we do not pose with the hips of Eve
I'll pat, play with, and pleasure my pussy
For it is the doorway to my ultimate power
It transmutes my pain into wisdom for my crown
I made a blood oath to love myself out loud
So, I'll be raunchy and rebellious
I will still be respected
and I'll very well do
whatever the fuck I please

KaSandra Turner

I want you on your knees
with your forehead rubbing my floor
I want your hands trailing towards my toes
My pretty little feet will step firmly
on the back of your head
Put this collar around your neck
Be my obedient little pet and I'll grace you
with a flash of light between my legs
Better yet, I'll chain you to my bed
and watch the sweat of your desires
drench into my sheets

I want your begging to ring through my ears
and leave lasting imprints like *Clair de lune*
Your chest lifting with excitement
knowing that you belong to me
awakens my appetite of dominating you
Let your filthy secrets be the tunes
I grind on your tongue to

When you see that black and red glass candle
burning and sizzling with Dragon's blood
Baby, don't touch it
Let the light lead you to my command
I thirst to see you rage with orgasms
at the sight of me rubbing my silky pearls

You are right to fall in love with me
For this is an eternal bond
Open your mind and I'll show you
why I love what I do to you

To Summon a Temporary Lover

On a Friday at midnight and or during a waxing moon, gather:

A charged sigil to summon a lover
A red marker, red pen, or red color pencil
Brown kraft paper
An envelope
A glass plate
A mortar and pestle
A red couples candle
A love spell oil
Catnip
Rose
Hibiscus
Cinnamon
Dragon's blood resin
A cigar (to burn tobacco smoke over the resins, herbs and flowers

Rub three drops of love spell oil in the palms of your hands. On the paper, respectfully address to whom you are writing the petition. State who the petition is for with their name and birth date. In this case, *your* information. Detail what you want from your lover, what they look like, how they treat you, what purpose they serve and how long you want to have them in your life. Be specific and write as if it has already manifested. Fold the paper three times towards you and place it in the envelope. Do not open the envelope once it is sealed.

Burn tobacco smoke over the herbs to awaken the spirits and over the candle. Thank the herbs for their service to you. With your dominant hand, add the herbs and a few drops of oil to the mortar and crush the ingredients with the pestle. Place the sigil on your altar and place the plate directly over it. Pour the crushed mixture on the clean, glass plate and leave a circle in the middle to place the candle in it. Anoint the candle with more oil from the base to the tip nine times towards you. Roll the candle in the mixture three times towards you. Burn the bottom of the candle over the plate until wax bleeds off. Place the candle in the circle of the plate and surround it with more of the mixture. With your lover on your mind, light the candle and say this spell out loud:

I light this candle, this flame to be
I call my lover unto me
The moon shines with my desire,
bring me passion as bright as fire
Lover, baby I call to you,
bring me lust and romance too
Do as I say and honor me,
this spell is cast
So let it be!

Once the candle and herbs have burned and the fire goes out, place the envelop in a place where it will be untouched and undisturbed. Once you have manifested your lover and your time with them is done, burn the petition and the envelope. Bury the ashes in the earth or offer them to the ocean.

What better way to see my dreams
unfold in this realm
than by rubbing all my private places
and drenching my sheets in sacred secrets?

What better way to pleasure myself
than by summoning my sensual cries
until I reach heaven and sing the songs
that reveal my greatest desires?

-Masturbate to manifest

KaSandra Turner

Sex Magick

We've been placid and patiently waiting
for precise planetary positions and alignments
for the perfect place and time to dive
into the lucidity of our wildest dreams
The moon,
bright and pregnant with our wishes
calls out to our seduced senses
on a Venus night —*and you're right where I want you*
Listen, I know you find yourself aroused in mystery
I can feel your eyes follow my strut to my altar
on the nights I work with catnip, hibiscus, and dried rose
I can feel it in my bones
You sizzle with curiosity when our gazes meet
You've said it before
You're tired from the ordinary life of work and no play
You're always left feeling depleted and drained
Feeling robbed of energy meant to fuel
your passions and visions
You yearn for a miracle
that will change the trajectory of your life

Well, here I am
poised patiently planted with pretty panties
peeking through my ankle length lavender laced robe
in the middle of my living room floor
My stillness calls your desires forth
Come to me
Follow my trail of cinnamon and cardamom
beauty oil baby

137

because I know you're ready to chain me to the wall

I'll meet you in the shower fully naked and lathered
Or would you rather
find a safe space in my stare
while your fingertips map my back line
after you've unhooked my lingerie yourself?
I know you love it when I scry into your eyes
Our moans and breaths begin to harmonize
while our body heat steams the bathroom
But there's no water running yet
Just the gushes of juices flowing from between my legs
slithering onto your fingers
and into the palms of your hands
Slide your fingers in my mouth
Show me why you wish to live in me
Let me taste the sweetness of my yoni
and rediscover why you feel so blessed and lucky
to flick and lick the fleshy fluorescent pink parts of me
Caress and bathe my beautiful brown body
Miss no marks and wipe every part of me clean
Let's baptize each other
and send our sins swimming away
leaving untainted purity

When we're wet, clean, and steaming
follow the trail of red, pink, and white candles
that light our way to sacred grounds
Let's summon the Gods and give them a show
Make them grant our wishes
and show them how humans do it

KaSandra Turner

Let's make the demons beneath our feet
thirst and rage at the sight of you bending me over
with my legs gapped and split like sliced peaches
Let's merge our power and passions
in the circle I casted, cause baby
I love it when you throw your head back
and hold the back of my head
when I'm grounded knees deep into the floor
Moan and grunt as I wave your wand
in and around my mouth and point it down
directing your masculine energy into me

And when I'm done performing my aria
from you thrusting your will in me,
darling let me taste your seeds
Enter the cosmos between my knees
Make our spirits intertwine infinitely
Stargaze through the portals of my eyes
We are light bodies ascending beyond space and matter
Interstellar travel through the abyss within me
as I pull, stretch and suck you into
my multidimensionality
Follow the rhythm in the flow of my hips
Let me smack my lips up and down your north node
Baby, lead us to divinity!

Focus on your deepest desires
as you coil into the vastness of my space
Immerse yourself and embrace the void
Know that the world, love, and healing is yours
when you submit to my sublime femininity

Hold me while we're under my spell
Excite those fallen angels in the realms of hell
Spread me open while the winds whirl
and I whine from you feeling so good
Make the messengers come soring down
cause we've been at it for hours
and the night grows nervous when I moan so loud
releasing my orgasm to the stars
My potions will come pouring on your lips and chin
Our lust, love, darkness, and sensuality will
merge, bend and be the reason
we transform and receive
all the ever-flowing rewards meant for us

And when we've stationed back on Earth
The candles will have fallen into slumber
Our bodies will be charged and linked
The heavens will have bowed to our prayers
My body will quiver vulnerably
in your divinely masculine hands
Come to me, sweet honey
I've been thriving to show you
how to have sex magick

For Witches with Periods

The blood is a sacred preservation of cosmic essence. This primordial fluid is a symbol of life and death; it is a sacred tool used to sustain and preserve life and can be used as a destructive weapon. It is a holy beacon of passion and power. To be born with it is the ultimate honor.

Although it is purged, period blood is the sacred life force that connects you to your divine feminine. Rituals during the monthly flow *enhances* a witch's work. To be in a potent state of receptivity is magical. To give an offering that is free flowing is enlivening especially since the flow is in sync with the moon.

Use it in your own workings and offer it to whom you wish under the knowing that consent has been given. Be mindful of who you offer your blood to and of how it is used. Sanitation and cleanliness is a nonnegotiable. Channel your desires. Visualize them as the light of your favorite color flowing out of you when you feel the blood gushing out. Send those wishes to the divine and witness how much your life changes.

Most of all, love it and embrace it. It is not possible without you, you sexy witch!

The Magick of Healing

My ritual is as unique
as the patterns on my fingertips
It is a sacred process
that allows me to unravel
stream and submerge in the overflowing ripples
of my divine intuition
imparted by the All

It is through my constant acts of devotion
to the oneness grander than my singular expression
that I emit and radiate the intensity
of an incessantly creating universe
that warps and merges into itself

I trace my reality from the pictures in my visions
bestowed by spirit to enhance my dream
I am rooted in my primal urge
to bend and bow at the feet of my desires
It is divine knowledge, reason and skill
that guide me during this sacred process
of manifesting my greatest wishes

The ritual is a sacred ceremony
where I honor all that I am

KaSandra Turner

Another Reason

Leather, mahogany, and vanilla trio and lift me
as your heart lights a fireplace in your chest
I discover myself softened when you sneak
kisses on my forehead and gift me memories
of our first date under Virginia's summer sunshine

My tongue races in excitement when I summon angels
to protect your soles as you pace atop the earth
My heart was antiquated and fossilized
before I realized your beaming brilliance bestowed
a seraphic gravity that gleams and glistens
life into things left drained and dried

I stared death in the nose as many times
as the count of hairs on my head
I even tried with my own might to meet my own demise
I refused to endure more loss and dread
So, I chose to conjure magick for our love instead

I scrubbed the trauma from my skin
until my bones burned clean
Wove life everlastings into my kinky goddess twists
I anointed a white couple's candle with a soul mate oil
covered it in calendula, rose and dried jasmine flowers
Burned frankincense and peony root in a cauldron
before the great Goddess and prayed on my hands and knees

Do you see, my sweet
how you ignite the light in my rituals?

That you are the reason for my humble prayers?
Place your ears on my pulsing bosoms
Let them share the trillion reasons
you inspire me to live again

Hands Vol. 1

I sometimes think that
I was born with the gift to give
That I was blessed with hands
that could wave and magically make love appear
in places that I could not imagine
With these hands I climb trees
that sky scrape galaxies
that lead me to plentiful possibilities
I gently conjure orgasms within my being
and have in men needing nourishment and healing
I mix soil and cement the grounds
that lead me to the morrow's moment
When time freezes like a possum in mechanic lights
my hands weave a portal,
an entrance to eternal life
These hands have hauled bags of bones
of my past lives to the bed of rivers
They have drowned them beneath the rocks
at the lows of the water's feet
and used my hair to dry them clean
These hands
Oh, these hands
that work my magick
are enchanted channels for source energy
They are the mediums between
me and my magick

Hands Vol. 2

I taste the world through touch
My fingertips converse with wise vines
from grand-momma willows
Their wisdoms flow through my palms
and gift me memories of the moments
I beamed down to earth
My hands soften my suffering
and paint my pain onto voids of white
They are the divine mediums between
my aching heart and the heavens
When my soul sends signals of sorrow
to my pulsing fingertips
I gently calm my sacred rivers
with heated palms to melt my iced cheeks
I burry them wrist deep
into the womb of the earth
as an offering in exchange for sweet salvation

My hands would ache for the wrinkled skin
under my granny's chin
Her joints showed me how far she'd been
She conjured beauty through the pound cakes she made
and we savored her smiles through the love she gave
I sometimes found myself grounded in grief
So, I'd hold my hands together in contrition
like folded craft paper with written intentions
to pray and send my thoughts to the all

Lift me up, ancestors

as I raise my hands up to you!
Help them to climb
beyond the chem trails and clouds
that cover my vision of the stars that guide me
Send healing through these hands
as they have withered away from your divinity
Hold them, beloved departed ones
Help them create and weave
what the tongue cannot articulate
Let them sink deep into my pits
and pull out the gunk that plagues my belly
For when I create
the life within me will move and flow
I will be whole, saved, and soothed again
And it is so

Our hands, you see
carry the journeys of our lives
and heal our aches
through all that we sew, sculpt and write
How blessed we are to have them
these wands and antennas
that release our fires and electricity
that mold and shift our realities
They will share the deepest parts of us
should we just trust in all that is divine

Feet

My feet ached from a million-mile journey
I walked with bare soles above coals of fire
Stomped rigid mountains with piercing points
that crucified me
I died a few times along the way
I panted forward with braids covering
my face from the whipping sun
My feet never crumbled
even with the stab and burn wounds
that dressed my toes and ankles

I grew restless one evening
when the crows started singing
My feet throbbed inside out
and my soles screamed to my soul for relief
through the holes the mountains left
I weakly crawled on my knees to my altar
with my hands gripping the edges
of my wooden table
with tears slapping my face
just as she did when I was eight

I slowly faded that night
as the cold mist kissed my forehead
and crawled through my lungs
Before my eyes retired,
a being stood staring
and covered me with wings

KaSandra Turner

that stretched across the room
Another at my feet
One being said to me,
I see the sorrow seeping
through your feet my sweet
You have bled out all your tragedies
on your way up north

The voice rang like the great bell Gabriel
and I knew this was an angel
The other a saint
And that saint sat still
and silently soothed my aches and burns
A bowl of blessed and lightly brewed lavender tea
was prepared for me
Sunflowers, chrysanthemums,
tulips, roses, and Florida water
danced and soaked my soles
Their majestic songs and radiant prayers
washed over me as I wept

Ode to my faithful feet
who have carried me along the way
who have rooted themselves into the earth
so that my crown may
extend towards stardust
and collect cosmic arrays of memories
of wholeness
They are stupendously fearless
to have paced through caves
and conquered defeat

I stand like oak trees due to their bravery
and they'll continue to carry me
another million miles

Recipe for a Foot Soak

Waters:
Spring water
Holy water
Florida water
Rose water

Salts:
Epsom Salt
Dead Sea Salt
Pink Himalayan Salt

Dried flowers & Herbs:
Rose buds
Lavender
Calendula
Jasmine
Echinacea

Fresh flowers:
Red, white and pink Rose petals
Chamomile
Sunflower Heads
Daisies
Peonies

Optional ingredients:
Agave or honey
Oat milk or other milk

These ingredients may also be used in a spiritual bath with the intention of being uplifted, light and magnetic.

The Magick of Healing

It is through overcoming my triumphs
that I embrace the infinite pleasures of the universe.

I rejoice in love and perfect trust.

I am my purest form of authenticity.

I am flourishing unapologetically
and with my own permission.

I AM an embodiment of divine love.

I confidently project my will
to illustrate and mold my reality.

I am that I am.

I AM MAGICK.

It is my deepest belief that magick can be defined as, *using the energies of the universe in conjunction with the will to create change and manifest. It is the will of the creator projected into the universe to co-create one's reality in the realm of the physical.*

May you always work your magick in a way that is authentic to you. I trust that your rituals serve you in the most divine ways. That they lead you to divine healing in every aspect of your life. May you be abundant in all the ways you wish to be.

And it is so.

Sacred Spaces

For every space we abandon, there remains a vengeful shadow waiting for our return. Some may even follow to haunt the new walls we discovered when we escaped what was left unhealed.

They whisper everything we believe to be our failures and claw out the lies we told ourselves as children. They chant all the spells we casted out of fear of being rejected by individuals who hate themselves. They remind us of our beliefs that we are meant to be bitter and unwavering.

Return to that space before you enter another. Embrace that entity, no matter how raging it may appear to be. It was birthed after you rejected the most beautiful aspects of yourself. It is everything you wish to express and be, freely. It is *you*. Return to *you*. Deem no part of you forsaken or unworthy.

Return to the home that you left out of self-pity, shame, regret, fear or rage. Lock pupils with yourself and remember that love is the node that will light the way. The sacred space begins with you. You are that sacred space. Enter it, under the condition that you have accepted what cannot be changed and are willing to weave new baskets that display your authenticity. Enter it, with the knowing that past regrets and mistakes are moments in time that do not define your future, but were a part of your journey of divine evolution.

You are sacred. Your body is sacred. Your art is sacred. Your voice is sacred. Your journal entries are sacred texts that tell the story of your odyssey. You are the perfect embodiment of light and darkness. May every ground you stand upon bow and be deemed sacred, as you are. Pardon yourself for accepting their unwelcome thoughts as your truth. The "safe space" they offered was nothing more than a prey ground made easy for their hunting. You are not responsible for their predatory behavior. They did what they believed to be right, so why not do what is truly spiritually aligned with you?

I know that this is may be difficult to swallow and many won't agree with this, but before you decide to do that vengeance magick, curse someone or hex them ask yourself: *what did I do to make them believe they had any right to disrespect me or overuse my energy? What did I say or do that gave idea that I welcomed their behavior? Did I set clear boundaries and put space between me and the individual(s)? Was I vocal and an advocate for myself? What can I do instead of taking this route?* Be sure to get a reading by an unbiased intuitive spiritual adviser, reader, channel and or intuitive before making such a decision to ensure that you are not needlessly putting yourself or others in harms way. Not guiding your anger and rage is a promised route to chaotic and needless destruction. You power is more potent and intense that you may think. Lastly, *your intention is everything.*

I welcome you into this sacred space to claim the healing that was robbed from you. You are here. I am here. We are here learning, growing, unraveling and finding our way back home together.

We set our intentions for the reciprocation
of the energy we give willingly
We tug at our galaxy in impatience
to form a reality
where we are given without judgment

A person shows up to open our doors
or pay for our coffee or tea at a parlor
they offer a helping hand
to place our groceries in our trunks
and we refuse, ever so politely
with smiles that conceal our wanting to receive
The universe conforms to our will

The *why* remains a mystery
Or is it just that we
are looking for the *bigger* things
as if the *little* moments hardly matter
They are the trial runs
that test our readiness
to humbly and gratefully receive
If we cannot welcome the little gestures
how can we, really
be open to the *greater* things?

When distance swallows us whole
and the winds carry us across the seas
it is you whom I will forever hold
within the deepest parts of me

KaSandra Turner

I possess a chainsaw for a tongue
I can cut trees from their roots with it
It can stretch around mount Everest twice
when I begin pouring out words of encouragement
I would rather stick it out and whip it
with a belt with blades sewn in
before I ever use its power
to destroy my neighbors again
They spat on me first
before they saw the scrapes they left
They noosed my heart and drug it
against the concrete on its bare skin
They laughed and mouthed up my tears
and spit them out

Twenty summers and winters flew in
My breasts, wrinkles and curves
had set into their new home
These memories sometimes knock at my door
wanting me to have those conversations
The giants rolled their eyes towards the ground
and stomp away from me
to avoid looking into their mistakes
Perhaps all they saw was a collection of nightmares
when they look upon my face
Although I can harness the power
of a million suns
I'd prefer to have those conversations
to release what's been done

I'll Make it One Day

The idea that I'm not worthy enough
bites down on my head
It chews my skull and brains
until they're ground into worthlessness
It spits my remains into the dirt
and the earth cries and shivers
from the sparks and sizzles
of my remains decaying into her pits

I itch to share my art in a world
that programs visions of me as a failure
into my psyche
They've convinced me that overproduction is key
and that key may not unlock the door
that will lead me to rainbows and purple lights
I saved up enough self-doubt and bought the lie
that as my body ages
I scare off the chances of success
That I should've started before I developed breasts
I wish to see seas of souls shining and crying
because my art has helped heal the places
others have hammered down to the ground
I ache to share my smile in a world
that tells me I must look like
unrealistic anime fantasies in real time
I must look like exotic dancers conserved
in a nun's garment to be taken seriously

I weep knowing that I choose

to keep my head buried into my computer screen
writing and rewriting for nonexistent hours
after homeschooling my children
I eat guilt for breakfast and shame for dinner
knowing that I sacrifice our moments
to create in hopes that
mommy's gifts will buy them train sets
puppies and mountain hauls of chocolate chip cookies
I sometimes hate myself for leaving my brothers and sisters
For seeing my mother in tears
because her grand-babies are not a hug away,
but two thousand six hundred and ninety-five miles
stretched across the country
She yearns to see her daughter live her dream,
but what is the dream?
A million followers on Instagram that I may never reach?
Performing my poetry on a yacht at sea?

I used to believe that art was a form of expression
and that the internet could be a space for us to share
our innermost thoughts and feelings creatively
I started believing that I must use my art
as a tool for competition
when it should be expressed to promote world unity
I'd rather wear a hat of integrity
and let it cover my face from a scorching sun of fame

I collect my tears in glass jars
to be charged under the moon
I share these wishes when she's pregnant
so that she'll birth my intentions

Like the shrubs in my back yard
growing through concrete
I'll gamble my chances of growth
and trust that I'll thrive in a world
where I can be cleared for the fuck of it

I don't wish to brand my life through aesthetics
for a social score that could be burned by
the toxins of cancel culture
Water doesn't drown itself
and I won't sink into my pessimism
believing that I won't make it in this world
Believing is the dream
That's what makes the world real

I'll eat the body of delusion
until I break through the confusion
of whether I'm worthy enough to share my work
I'll spread my words
like pollen riding the backs of bees
to be dispersed in gardens
for the emergence of plants and plum trees
I'll have a forest filled with my art collections
and share them as offerings to humanity
Their smiling faces and raining eyes
are the best surprises
I could ever hope for

KaSandra Turner

Sister Healers

There was something magical about my sisters
The way they would transfer their love into my scalp
when they braided my hair
I'd sit with my chest towards the sky in their chairs
A calming sense of peace flowered from my crown
with each braid that wrapped around my head
like Saturn's rings
They danced with the wounds of my shadows
Tears would come marching towards my ears
because I was swarmed with warmth that beamed
from the spaces where they saved a seat for me
They anointed between my coils with oils
and they seeped deep into my Sahasrara
I'd offer poems of wisdom in exchange
for the light they had given me

Our laughs would ring for hours
We danced on rainbows
sored through lightening and fought with thunder
We lifted the anchors from our secrets
and cried with each breath of release
We purged and casted circles during the witching hour
and casted spells to tame our demons
We unraveled our toughest layers
with each braid they took down
They may not know, but they were gifted at reiki
I felt love and cosmic energy enter me
when they rubbed their fingertips through my strands

It was more than a braiding session
Love lifted its beautiful wings
in those sacred spaces
I am eternally grateful
for the kindness they shared
on the days they braided my hair

KaSandra Turner

Having to parent yourself in ways
your parents failed to
needs to be a part of healing conversations
With the anger, without the sarcasm
With the tears, without the blaming and child blaming
We need you, parents
to know how you harmed us
To know how you've hurt and abandoned us
when we needed you in those moments
We are not your slaves ,
yet we were beaten with belts and switches
and other things you can name
Including the wrath of your words

Past lives of slavery replayed in our dreams
when you beat us to bed
We did not incarnate to be imprisoned again
We came back to find love
Another life to free us from former whips
It felt like the chains we broke
found our wrists and stretched into this life
at times when you beat your frustrations on us
We grew like fruits with deformities

We were not meant to be your outlets
yet you bestowed tragedies upon us
of being one anyway
We have grown in our awareness
We've found our self-love
and we need you to know
the damage that you've done

The Magick of Healing

I love how patient you are
with your grand-babies
The rivers must be proud
of your softness and submission
May I have a little taste from your fountains?
I'm parched
I've grown into a desert
with my waters buried beneath my grounds

Dig a pit into my earth
Show me where you left
the streams I've needed
Show me where to find a drink
I'd prefer it be poured from your eyes

Mother Dearest,

There were times where I feared you. I would swallow my tongue to prevent your wrath. I tried to express myself as a young woman, yet I was greeted with the shame of feeling at times. I understand that the women in your family never taught you softness. You had to fend for yourself for so long that your default settings changed from optimistic to dominating. Communication was your nemeses; you did not get upset, you raged. It was difficult to see past the smoke of your volcanoes at times.

It's unfortunate that you have a gigantic heart that gives and pours relentlessly all to feel depleted afterwards. I was confused at one point because I could not fathom for the life of me how you gave endlessly and appeared to be so angry all the time. It took me a while, but it finally clicked; you just needed someone to hear and see you. Your anger was a mask for your hurt. You were not always angry. You were tired. You needed help. To be loved unconditionally. You were betrayed by the people you trusted most and when you expressed yourself you were seen as the offender. What you endured in your past isn't fair and we will get through it if that is what you need. Although I will not excuse you for the moments you hurt me, I am actively choosing to understand and help in all the ways I can. You see, you birthed a healer. It is because of you that I believe we birth the healers we need in this world.

The trauma that ran through our family was normal until it met me. I will continue to show up and make you proud of all the reasons why you chose to keep me despite being told to abort. It is because of your sacrifice that I am here.

I hope that my art can give us a break one day. I will carry this hope beyond the moment the last leaf on earth falls. I will forever love you, Momma. We'll get better one day. I believe it.

Some of our parents have seen hells
that some of us cannot imagine burning in
They still choose to show up
with blood rusted armor
half sliced swords and tarnished helmets
even when they feel they've failed
When the chance to love softly flows away
like wet sand in a fractured hand
they still show love in the best ways they can

I choose to show as much grace as I can
Beneath their raging seas of howls
and wraths of winds
lies a treasure chest filled
with the gold, coins and jewels
buried away in their childhood
They cannot give what they never received

I will welcome love and boundaries when needed
and show up in a way that I need
I'll allow this energy to bleed into their skin
and let it wrap around their bodies
like ribbon around a present
For it is a gift to love in spaces
where hate, pain and sorrow exist
I will pour the purest waters of wisdom
out into the streams of their hearts
This trauma ran in the family
until it foolishly
ran into me

When I took off my mask for the first time
I was instantly shot into the macrocosm
I was undressed of all the temporary roles
that concealed my truth
It was the first time I felt
the striking bliss of peace

KaSandra Turner

If only we remembered how deeply we can love
in the moments our words begin battling for thrones
If only we remembered that our words are seeds
that can be planted into the grounds of each other
Perhaps we are fully aware and choose to plant
what will grow along our neighbor's back
to break their spines
because we feel spineless in the moments
where anger rings a vengeful beat

How often must we take for granted
the moments we have together
and choose cancel culture over climbing mountains
that block our vision with their heights?
The beautiful thing about mountains
is that although they are firm and unmovable
they can be climbed
with the will and determination
that measures beyond an angel's crown
We can immerse ourselves
and marvel in the way
they shoot out from the earth
Defensiveness is sometimes
a lazy route to understanding
and suppresses our ability to be receptive

We tend to our plants with respect
and a calmness orchestrated by God herself
We flower, vulnerably and are free of shame
when our mouths spill our truths to our pets
because judgment doesn't shine in their eyes

Yet we knock the ladders from under another's feet
When will we learn that we are in a shared dream?
That we can collectively reshape reality?
We are a universal family
whose origins begin and never ends
in the stars
We are stronger as a unit
than when we are apart

Throat Chakra Affirmations

On a Wednesday evening, cleanse a blue glass candle with Florida water. Light the candle and speak these affirmations out loud:

I listen attentively before I speak.
I honor silence to welcome in peace.
I communicate clearly and choose my words wisely.
I am honest with myself and vocalize the things I need.
I respectfully communicate to my ancestors and guides.
I use the power of my voice to set clear boundaries.
I ask questions to gain divine clarity.
I am honest in my interactions.
I engage in healthy conversations.
I speak with courage and confidence.
I honor my daily oral hygiene as a sacred ritual.
I honor my integrity and speak highly of myself.
I am free of gossip and control my tongue.
I speak my desires into existence with confidence.
I speak my truth daily in abundance.
I give others the space to be themselves.
I speak love over myself daily in abundance.
My words are spells that encourage healing and balance.

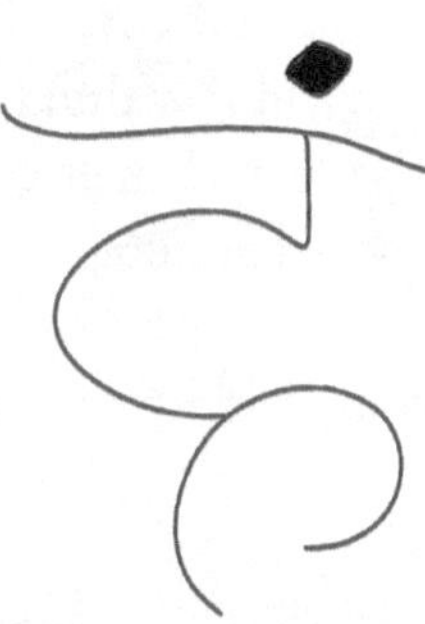

Pawpaw's Peach Cobbler

I miss the way my grandfather
would skin fresh peaches
and let them soak in sugar water
He'd boil them in cinnamon
butter
sugar
nutmeg
and a secret spice that
always soothed the wounds I carried
to their home during the holidays
He had shelled walnuts for knuckles
after being shot and left for dead
I never tasted the trauma
in his hand made bread

He buried World War II on the battle field
and traded PTSD for dinners,
ministry and praise with his family
I always saw sugar seep through his smiles
when the grandchildren gathered
and begged granny for cakes and candy before dinner
I, the eldest and mighty ring leader
ignorant and pure ensured
we feasted and were drunk in delight
He was patient when placing
the uncooked breading
and peaches in the buttered glass baking dish
He'd let his masterpieces marry and bake together

My mouth would cry for a taste before it emerged
We'd sit bonded on the couch
as old westerns played in grey
We'd sit and wait for his love to bake
Memories of his childhood
would claim the atmosphere
and my past pleads and screams from beatings
would release their grip over my being

After he plated the cobbler, he'd bless it
and it magically became more sweet
more decadent, slightly savory
and fulfilling
as if it marinated in his wisdom
and in the love of the God he prayed to
The vanilla ice cream would melt atop the cobbler
like my heart when he'd carry me,
when the heat of the flavors he combined dissolved
onto my pallet
I would whirl into a dimension
filled with his life lessons and legacy
and in the smiles he shared
when he and my grandmother
homed me during my first two years of life
He was my second father
An angelic saint sent
to engrave his heart in mine

He took his full recipe
with him to his grave
and all I hold now are the memories

of what he did for me on the days
he made peach cobbler

Trees

I marvel at the trees when their leaves
tickle traces of their wisdom in the skies
I can't deny I sometimes see
the divine in the sway of their vines
You ever just sit and soak in the sunshine
and breathe beneath the leaves of a tree?
You ever just felt the need to embrace
their trunks and release past pain and memories?

It's something about their calming presence
that keeps me calm and connected in the present
They see all things and judge not a flaw in my thoughts
They just...
let me be and bestow their blessings of harmony
Their roots pulse and never miss a beat beneath me
I envy their ability to connect with their community
Even on the days it rains
they stand unified and embrace the shaking storms of change

I often wonder how far and deep their roots reach
Do they stretch so low that they coil Hades's throne
and cool the heat from his feet?
Do they glow and form ley lines to guide the eyes of Persephone?
How proud they must be to shake the hands of God almighty
Even when they bend in the winds
breaking doesn't come so easily
What a wonder it is to be at the lows of their heights
and experience the flight of their majestic rhythm

The Magick of Healing

I used to envy the way they stood in their authenticity
Attracting the birds, butterflies and the bees
Trees don't attempt to control
or wonder and worry about what is
They connect with one another through root systems unseen
I guess this means that there's a lesson there for humanity
Love and connect to yourself
Pour love into your community

I appreciate plants, flowers, and trees. Watering them is a ritual I cherish; I give unto nature as she gives unto me. To love and care for these sentient beings with personality is such a blessing. I don't have to worry about being judged for embracing my body hair and stretch marks. They remind me that I am never alone. How could I be when they are reflections of wisdom and inner peace? They just sit and bask in their own wisdom and beauty.

Nature is exemplary in her ability to welcome me and honor my humility when I'm experiencing her presence. I'm greeted with cool breezes tickling my knees and elbows while the sunshine beams between tree branches and dancing leaves. The turtles pop their heads out of the womb of the lake to greet me in curiosity. They remind me to be curious and open to the wonders of life. To flow and ground myself to leave a gateway open for balance. They remind me to honor my intuition and emotions in a practical way that supports my growth and evolution. I always hear opera songs when the cardinals and blue jays sing to the instrumental of winds carrying dead leaves across the grounds. The crickets and bugs join and they all sing as a choir. It's a meritorious experience that leaves a profoundly lasting imprint on my soul.

Nature is the one place where I'm guaranteed to be my most vulnerable self without fearing the wrath of exacerbating judgment. I am free to plunge into introspection and not feel forced to harshly criticize myself for the unfavorable thoughts that emerge.

The most amazing part is feeling loved and connected to myself and the Source greater than my own personal existence. There are no interferences or fears from the ongoing static and buzzing from the outside world. I cherish and honor this special space and sometimes wish to never leave her sublime embrace. This is why I choose to remember that I am every bit a part of her. I love Mother Nature and therefore love myself to the same degree.

To My Innocence

Because no one has the heart to do it, let me peer into the depths of you. You were bullied. Physically, verbally and sexually abused. You received no justice and are healing alone. Others can't perceive past their own ignorance and this isn't your fault. I know it's difficult, but please don't take this personal, my love. Don't hold yourself responsible for their mistakes.

Your mother is wounded, traumatized, alone and afraid. Your father is searching for his honor. But, please remember that you are accompanied by an infinitesimal count of clusters faithfully shining to guide you to your own brightness to ensure your safe passage home. God is within you. I am the future you who has witnessed the richness and fullness of your life. Your strength is rooted in passion. Molded and sculpted from love and compassion. You evolved so purely through your art that your words became a beacon of light that led others to their healing. You surpassed the success you believed you couldn't achieve.

Despite the fear and tears that swallow your being, you conjure love and project it into the world. How magical and immense is your strength! Although your heart aches to be understood and treated with reverence, you'll transcend beyond your suffering. You'll grow deeper into your intelligence; you'll be known as one who merges the arts of poetry and magick.

You are the purpose and one day when you least expect it, you'll wear your honor as the crown you deserve. Stay confident, grounded and express your gratitude for the little things. Before you know it, you'll fly. You are capable, disciplined, trustworthy, honest, authentic, and divinely intuitive. Continue sharing your art. You encourage peace and harmony to flow within you and in the world.

I love you, star beam.

KaSandra Turner

Sestina of Shadowed Dreams

The sting filled stories I tell the pregnant moon
seem to suffice, awakening waves in the waters
The willows, wise and still, wrap their songs around my heartbeats
They rush to dust away my sorrows of tomorrow
Shrubs tickle my soles to offer me comfort
They all dance in symphony attempting to arouse my dreams

Agony joyfully crawls through the abyss of these dreams
During these nights the stars sway around the moon
Memories of shadows consume my comfort
The same shadows who rage war with the waters
They whisper, *I'll crunch on your cries again tomorrow*
Their haunting laughs devour my heartbeats

Willows whip my heels down my avenue of shattered heartbeats
I mourn as my thorns are surfaced in this realm of dreams
My eyes sparkle with fear of meeting tragedy again tomorrow
So, the stars stretch their shine, guiding my gaze to mother moon
She cradles my storms as her reflection seduces the waters
They shelter and nest a home in my comfort

But at what price is the cost of my comfort?
At what speed is the need of my heartbeats?
How do I manage to mirror murky waters?
I presume it depends on the mood of my dreams
I am pushed to find my strength by a crescent moon
So that fireflies may light me a path to tomorrow

Crisp winter skies carry my trembling knees to tomorrow

The Magick of Healing

I seek shelter in my shadows behind the blazing sun's comfort
Instead, I find her singing, that beautiful pregnant moon
Her opera singing craters twine ease around my heartbeats
I surrender to her grace in the center of my dreams
as I float face down kissing the face of the waters

At that place where the shore meets the feet of the waters,
I discover the pacing prints of tomorrow
Freed of the screaming shadows of my dreams,
I roll in the sandy arms of comfort
Steady and graceful are the songs of my heartbeats
as they are birthed from the skies behind the sparkling moon

My nightmares of dreams are cleansed by holy waters
I rejoice, refreshed under the dazzling moon of tomorrow
The stars, shrubs and willows sing and comfort my heartbeats

Pink peonies dance
Their perfume and petals fly
freely in the skies

A cousin is the first childhood friend,
a sibling birthed from another mother.
They are like blueberries, me the raspberry.
We are uniquely different
but play well together.
Although my cousins and I
have branched away
to different fields and forests
because time and experience tarnished our roots
I choose to hold the memories
of our first laughs together.

We are one within our family tree
and I know that one day
we'll return in harmony.

KaSandra Turner

When They Don't See You

The value of life should not be weighed against
gold or silver. They are tangible, yet lack feeling flesh.
The value of life should not be
determined by the mood of someone
for a moment that will evaporate
in little time.

Look to them not for the fortune of validation.
For they will betray you
should your lips not shimmer or shine.
Should you not be worthy to exist before their eyes.
They will snuff the light from within your pits
if you allow them.
Their compassion may end where they believe
your conventional beauty begins.
If so, their world may not be yours to exist in.

Your gold is not spun from the heat of their palms.
Your rhythm does not sway
to the off-beat of their drums.
If they measure your value or the quality of your life
against your physical attributes
pity them. —*They* have not yet awakened from the illusion.
Treating you as filth for not meeting *their* measurements
is an exposure of their false sense of self-worth and control.
It is a slap in the face of God
for not admiring the beauty in her diverse style of creation.
They have been petrified and zombified
with their ability to think freely dissipated and vanished.

A moment never returning.
If they see you solely through their pupils
they are easily tricked and fooled.
To pay them in self-hate is as equally foolish. —*You are sacred.*

You are the art that beams beyond their perception.
Submit not to their lack of empathetic intelligence.
The true form of your nakedness is angelic.
I marvel, bravely smiling
when I gaze upon you in the stars.
They are not your God.

    —Your worth rests *amidst your own hands.*

KaSandra Turner

Unsheltered Shadow

A sudden dread demands the silent atmosphere to flee
The walls grow weary and hide behind a dense energy
I feel my shadow silently creeping
through the crack in my door
and her whispers begin crawling up my chest
I open the door and prepare a seat
to the chair right of me in my prayer room
I light ten white candles cleansed in salt water
and seal the windows with black salt with more white candles
The stretch of her mouth towers my existence
Scratching screams escape her lungs
and her rage rapes the room
My candle flames fight with her waves of anger
I kneel to her howls in a fright that gusts my lungs
I too mourn for I know she needs nurturing

Her tears run red and her eyes glow white
I sit with seas in my own eyes waiting
for the screaming to simmer
She spits
The glass of doubts
I forced into her belly caught up to me
The glass cuts my face leaving scars
that paint me in the scabs of our past
She hates me for having pumped her full
of doubts, I can'ts, and I won'ts
She slaps me with the claws I created
and sends me into memories
of us in elementary

The Magick of Healing

There were days I would stare into a mirror steaming
and screaming I hated her for making me a target
For being dissimilar
bigger and darker than the other girls
For possessing emotional intelligence beyond our years
For having the wits and creativity of a whole class combined
I despised her for not fitting in to shoe sizes
meant for size four feet
I convinced her that she was nothing
disgusting
dishonorable
disgraceful
I cursed her with a tongue thorned with spikes of disdain
and declared that loss and dread
were her only reasons for living
She grew to believe
that everyone's life would be beautifully easy
should she die and leave no traces or memories
No funeral
No wake
And if they were kind enough to bury her
the casket would be better off closed
Cremating her remains would be better suiting
for a bastard beastling

I embrace the raging pain
before my throat is slain
She chokes my last tears out of me
when suddenly,
her grip loosens like petals falling off flower heads
The more I listen, the stronger the rivers

race down her frightening frame
Her wolf like cries transition into mine
One song into another
The candles and walls grow still
witnessing the fight of her will
ease and melt as harmony becomes her

She haunted me over the years
because I wasted our tears
cleansing others who believed they were impeccable
She wanted no waters from their sinks,
but to drink of the waters waving within me
My shadow was my nemesis
I have now welcomed her home
as a part of me

The Magick of Healing

Hold me until my nose runs dry
Untie my knots of faults
and bind my sins
Tie a bow with silk fibers around my chest
and remind me that I am a gift,
that this moment is temporary
Reveal the harsh truths of my internal sabotage
Make the sadness burn away like salt to a slug
Let your comfort be the lady bug
that rests gently on leaves
Remind me that you are here hearing me

Protect me in your supporting love
while your eyes unwind my fears
like wine creeping in from over poured glasses
Let me know we're bonded, hand in hand
on this journey of gain and loss
grief and gratitude
rising and fumbling
hate and love
The only space I feel safe to unravel
is in your arms
May we pour the hurt out from our eyes
A tear for a tear,
my dearly trusted friend

When we honor Earth Mother
by keeping her waters pure
by planting seeds to attract the bees
throw our trash away and even eat green
it is not just ourselves and her womb that we honor.
We hold space and respect all life on her surface.
We offer love and reverence to our animal friends
and send healing to our human family.
Like the ivy that clings and crawls
up the walls of our houses
we grow patience that extends towards
nebulae and celestial gas bodies.
As within, we connect with our higher selves.
So without, that connection is spread
amongst our cosmic communities.
More exists beyond our own picket fences.

-We are all that we have

The Magick of Healing

It is impossible to hold
the weight of the globe
with two shoulders
We would shrivel
and our bones would ache and crack with failure
But if we stood beside one another
shoulder to shoulder
hand in hand
spells to spells
heads held to the heavens
how high would we carry one another?

I'm willing to bet,
with my last breath
we would bulldoze the barriers
of limitation
Illusions of separation would shatter
Our individual uniqueness would matter
The Earth would weep wonders of green
and the planets would be our witnesses
God would cry cause her children have learned
the power of togetherness

-*Community matters*

KaSandra Turner

When Nature Speaks

I closed my windows to keep the wind out
It rang my doorbell
Come out, it whispered
I've got songs to sing for your ears only
I huffed and placed on my dirty running sneakers
The ones with the chewed shoestrings my cat left me
The ground shook in annoyance
Take off those barriers! It shouted
The grass awaits your naked feet
The sun sat on his thrown in the sky
He watched me shrug and drag my feet to the dirt
The grass raised like hairs on the back of necks
and on legs not shaven for weeks
The grass pulsed with every step I took
and the further I walked
the more my stress stressed itself to death
The wind sang secrets between my fingers
and lifted me above my worries
We cost nothing to love and help you
yet you pay for your death with disease,
dysfunction and disharmony
Just relax and breathe me in
Pull in the embrace of a tree
and see how much better off you'll be
You cry for sacred spaces
while we exist right before your faces
You trade vitamin D for the light in your phone screen
and fight against one another
as if you are true enemies

I frowned at the accuracy
Come to me, nature said as I wept
Tell me about your dreams

Root Chakra Affirmations

On a Saturday night, cleanse a red or brown glass candle with Florida water. Light the candle and recite these affirmations out loud:

I am present in the moment.
I am safe and grounded in my body.
I am connected to myself and the vibration of the Earth.
I honor the earth daily in abundance.
I am centered and balanced in tumultuous energy.
My body is a sacred temple and I honor it daily in abundance.
I am free of greed.
I eat and indulge in moderation.
I am wealthy because I am healthy.
I am calm and patient with myself and my progress.
I am secure in my home and am abundant in wealth.
I have a healthy relationship with my family.
I am firm with my boundaries.
I have healthy boundaries with those I love.
I adapt to change.
I accept my progress and trust that I am evolving.
I am practical and knowledgeable.
I have access to all resources that aid me in my success.
I am safe to experience security.
I am safe and secure within myself.

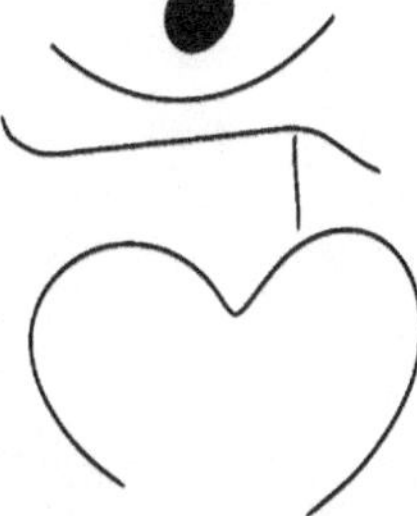

Darling,
no amount of wands
spells
curses or hexes
can ever enchant us apart
How can they
when we *are* the magick?

KaSandra Turner

We sometimes spend
mountainous amounts of moments
in our lives
searching for something enchanting
as if the fairy tale
doesn't exist within us already

-You are love

Love Me Like it Doesn't Hurt

I want you to rub your thumbs on my nipples
the way you scroll up and down your phone screen
Hold me like nests in trees
I'll lay secure in your branches of arms
Pick me up softly
like clouds of cotton candy
Taste me so I'll melt in your mouth
Scoop and grip my behind
Let me know you crave this body

Kiss me
like dawn dew drops on flower petals and leaves
fresh and soaking in a summer breeze
Just don't leave
after autumn, winter or spring
Stay here, baby
Let the moonlight shine through our sheer curtains
Feel me slowly swaying on you
beneath you
Let's merge with our chests pressed against each other's
I'll swallow your breath
while your lips quiver onto mine
I'll suck your bottom lip
as your fingers slip
between my yoni lips and thighs

Show me how gently you can love me
with words of affirmations
while you make love to me

I've been at the hardened feet of anger
and have confused impatience with love
Baby, it scares me
Can I cry in your arms and release the beatings
that struck me to stone?
Will your hands print up my back
and heat to incubate me?
I yearn to hatch and just be
But honey,
this world has been so cruel to me

Need me like early birds
catching the first of crawling worms
Cascade me
like the waking sun over my rooftop
kissing and hugging my body in the risings
Sing me soft tunes
like bubbling waves on sand
Hold my hand while you stare into my eyes
Let your soul shine me to sleep
I'll feel safe in your sacred space
Make me believe in love again

Safe and Sacred

I love to feel your eyes pinned on my body
when I'm deep within a trance
in the middle of my circle casted at 3am,
my body brimming with interconnected consciousness.
I striptease for the pulsing, dark abyss
as it sits gapped open during my performance.
Smoke rises to the heavens. The angels secretly grow curious.
My openness exposes your peeking eyes.

The darkness offers its security and welcomes me
while a voluminous glow claims the night.
God waits patiently for my petitions
to be burned in the womb of my cauldron.
Mother Crone cackles when you drool for my nakedness
to be entangled and intertwined in yours.
My black and red candles whip and seduce
my bottom painted with your palm prints.
My fingers summon your quivering knees.
They command them to kneel, —*even if they break*.
I stand over you, my hands caressing my breasts.
Both of my heels at each of your sides.

Fear does not exist in this place.
For sex is a sacred process of creation.
It is a raw expression of untamed passions
guided by divine minds, to transcend limitations.
Sex is connecting to our highest divinity
through fleshy bodies vibrating with sensations.
It is pleasure while manifesting safely in a sacred space

where the thoughts of poisoned minds do not exist.
I'll continue chanting until the clouds orgasm
releasing reigns of healing waters
that wash away my sigils drawn with white chalk.
My intentions will be sacred texts in Mother's grimoire.

The white spills through the tip of your wand
and I know that I have granted you
the comfort of freedom to release your wants to God,
—*let the embarrassment evaporate into oblivion.*
This is not the place to whimper with uncertainty.
We *are* God cumming and coming to our senses.
We are free and safe to experience our magick
and what it means to reclaim our power again.
We need no permission, but our knowing and truth
that this world will bend, so as our minds shift.
Let us unravel in our sacred space
so that divinity becomes us once more.

I Choose to Love Myself

I refuse to hate myself
into an appearance unfamiliar to me
I will stand against anything and anyone
who tells me to despise my body
until it's more shapely and socially acceptable
I'll be as sturdy as the undisturbed mountains
you can't pierce, push, or pull
I choose to love myself
while melting the fat off
like pistachio ice-cream running down a comb
in mid-July
I will caress my skin
until the acne is smoothed over
I will vibrate at a frequency
that shatters the toxins out of my body
I will not be manipulated
into believing that
I must hate and break my body down
as if love will not heal these bones
I love myself enough to know my faults
I honor myself enough to do and be better
I refuse to pay you in self-hate
I'd rather enrich myself with acceptance
appreciation
attention
and affection
I am a beautiful soul
and it will be seen through my skin
You'll feel it first

cause I've got a world within
waiting to be born

I Will Always Love My Sisters

Sisters, we have distanced ourselves
Thirteen summers have tiptoed away
and left us searching
for the promise rings we made
during our dates and baby doll meetings
Do you remember, sisters
the sound of our tea glasses clinking?
Our sips of faucet water burning our lips
as we imagined ourselves as rich
hot babes?
We made our first cakes
in those easy bake ovens
back when we bonded through
laughs and the lights of our imaginations

Come back home, sisters
Life has crunched on our spines
and left us bent and hunched back over time
Let us unwind
through the indulgence of cheese, chocolate
crackers and wine
Let us fill our bellies
with the stories that leave us gasping for air
Let's share the laughter
that holds our cheeks hostage

I miss the sight of light shining
through your eyes
I see that your glow now beams

through the cracks formed from
you piecing yourself back together
Let's dance and mold one another
Your hair in my hands,
mine in yours
in this space free of judgment
pity
hate
shame
Let us reclaim the letters we left
at the doorsteps of our little hearts
before we walked through the doors of life

I have always loved you
and that love remains
rooted like Redwoods, grounded and firm
Let's come back home
and dwell in this loving space
because you will always be my sisters
even when the last branch breaks

Working with the Heart Space

On a Friday evening, light a green (or pink) pillar or glass candle cleansed with salt water and Florida water. Light the candle and recite these affirmations:

I express gratitude for myself, others and for what I experience.
I am one with the omnipotence of the universe.
I am surrounded by love daily in abundance.
I radiate love daily in abundance.
I am free to love myself and others unconditionally.
I respect myself and welcome in healthy love.
I am protected with safe and necessary boundaries.
I am tapped into the wisdom of my emotions.
I am free of suffering and welcome in joy.
I am rooted and grounded in compassion.
I consciously choose love over fear.
I am honest about my emotional needs.
I show myself grace to raise my self-esteem.
I am emotionally independent.
I am emotionally intelligent.
I accept myself and welcome change.
I love myself in my totality.

KaSandra Turner

When You See Me

When you see me sick and throwing up my intestines
like porridge overflowing in a pot on high
do not fix your lips to ask if I am well
Fetch me a towel and hold back my hair
Let me dispel the food I craved all day

When you see that my feet have swelled with aches
like a puppy's nose to a bee sting
do not ask if there is a chair I am needing
Offer to carry me to a velvet cushion
filled with clouds, feathers and cotton
The cotton my ancestors picked for clothing
When you see that my hands hold my globe of a belly
cause it is filled with the world I am creating
do not assume that your hands are welcome
Marvel in my beauty and send me smiles instead

When that sacred river flows down my legs
my nose flares and my eyebrows fly
call the army of my mothers and sisters
Gather calendula, roses, jasmine and lavender
herbal blends, candles and incense
Cleanse the space and fill a pool with water and flowers
Pray to my ancestors who used hot towels
and the power of their tongues they used to move the winds
They will calm my body as I exit its bounds
They will fill the room with their songs and psalms
Those saints will protect the space from harm

The Magick of Healing

Before I go I will growl, groan and moan
Cause my hips will have spread like butter on bread
Surges of fire will contract my womb
and help push out that curly haired bundle
Don't you dare tell me to lay on my back
I will squat and birth on my hands and knees
They have already robbed me twice of my right
to birth naturally using my breath and feminine power
Higher-self willing, I'll have my chance again
Don't ask me if I need a white man
to deliver my baby as if his body
will be milked to feed my baby from his breasts

When you see me exhale from delivering my baby
and catch her with my own two hands,
do not crowd me
like fluoride eyes around a caged chimpanzee
Do not intervene like nosy Rose down the street
Cheer me on and howl to the moon
For life has entered this dream through me
I have given life from my own body
For I have birthed a miracle that even angels envy
I have become a mother for the first time again

When you see that snot has claimed my nose
and tears have raced down to that pool of water,
do not ask if I am distraught
Form a chain sealed with the shimmer of gold
with your fingers knotted into each other
Lift me with the breath of your prayers
Trust and know that I am fulfilled

Let me bask in the moment of my dream.

211

The Magick of Healing

You treat my people as though we are savages
You dug a hole in the earth
to create an ocean of our blood
We welcomed you
and you thanked us by high jacking our resources
the wombs of our women
the innocence of our children
the might of our men
You systematically created concrete cages
and developed a system that
you control to keep us poor
You renamed us as many times
as eons of winters passing
to keep us locked and looped
hunting for our identities
Our needs you ignorantly ignore

Now, we have our feet upon your necks
because we have disenchanted ourselves
We have awakened from your spells
We are uprooting your traditions
of conquering and slaughtering
You cannot flee; you are beheaded by your sins
We have noosed you to the debts you owe
They will be paid to those
whom you have conquered and controlled
You have been betrayed by your thievery
You will NOT stop this elevation
We are joining forces against you
Your fate is sealed
Your tail is tucked between your trembling knees

because you and I know
that as the volcanos bubble and rumble
humanity is awakening
You're scared shitless
because you know that we've already won

The dark is a sacred space that guided me to the liberation of my most authentic self. Darkness revealed the sum of insecurities and failures I cloaked and covered to invisibility. These spaces are filled with the wisdoms that carried me throughout my journey of self-discovery and self-acceptance. When others discarded, rejected and ignored my existence I was left to the depths of my own subconscious. The rejected parts of my individuality, extraordinary uniqueness and innocence were the dimensions I was awarded to explore. I was accompanied by the many layers of my own presence. The further I traveled through these hidden chambers the more I unraveled and demolished outdated beliefs of a world where I was limited and anchored from unconditional love. It was through reflection and introspection that I merged to one with my demons. I discovered that these demons did not torment me for control or to wreak destruction and chaos in the world. These beautiful beings were desperately reminding me of what needed addressing and healing. The darkness only revealed the truth of my power and potential and never casted judgment against my flaws and failures. I was often comforted with silence and the many voices of God that whispered songs of reverence to my soul. This space is sacred because my redemption was birthed upon the surrender of my egoistic fight to be recognized, validated and loved.

The void is a womb space where all waves of thought and light exist. It is a healing space where growing life is nurtured with no attachments of expectations, beliefs, limitations or instructions. It is full of pure, untouched life force energy. Do we not begin within the dark womb of our mothers? Do seeds not sprout from the dark pits of soil? I have learned along this path that this space contains all things and is even the source of all energy. It is neither good nor bad. It is the divine feminine space that births all things into creation. By exploring the sacred womb space of darkness, I have discovered that we will become whole once we merge our contraries.

The darkness will forever be a sacred space for me. I welcome her as she leads me to my light.

Your suffering and traumatic experiences led you to your magick and sacred spaces. You were devoted to healing through your craft. Now, let's have those conversations for the sake of healing.
It's time.

Healing

I placed my right foot halfway into a river
The other rested gently on its bed
I slowly raised my right hand
and wrapped ripples of stars around my wrists
as the darkness spilled across the heavens
My left hand extended into Earth Mother's belly
My skin shivered
My soul pulsed
Serenity silently slithered up my spine
and found its way to my crown
glowing golden with a holy shine
I faced my closed eyes
down into the resting river
and heard the spirits speak,
Come now, dear
Baptize yourself clean

KaSandra Turner

Returning to MySelf

I stood and gawked at my glowing reflection
in the mirror of my newly decorated bathroom
I closed my eyes and peered into the void
beneath my eye lids in wonderment
It blinked back in silence, staring and revealing
my own inner shadows
My hands, tingling and trembling with excitement
found themselves gliding along the rivers of my womb
I pressed my palms into my center
Indigo strings of lights formed along my surface
like nerves and veins atop the ground from old trees
It was the first time in years that I deeply breathed

I slowly swayed my head, forming an enthralling horizon
My knee length passion twists waved like vines
on a willow tree, trancing and captivating me
I found my hips slowly and sensually
mixing and grinding like a mortar and pestle
My tears were melting snow in spring
revealing hearts of pink and green

Divine wisdom and the knowledge of a million owls
coiled up from my root and extended itself
out of my head and presented me a crown
It gleamed with sparkling gloss and was jeweled
with the prizes that came after surviving the trauma
that consumed and spit me out in disgrace
The last of rustic blood raced from my earnest eyes
I rubbed my stretch marks and spoke out loud,

The Magick of Healing

I forgive you self, for the times you denied your truth
For forgetting your numinous luminosity
You are a portal that guides souls into this world
to observe, evolve and experience this reality
It was you who carried and provided for two bodies
at once for nine months and bounced back mentally
You nurtured yourself and found softness where it died
You poured the healing waters of your tears
over the wounds that scarred, calloused, and covered your heart

Despite your traumas, tribulations, and torments
you effortlessly extended ethereal energy
and exponentially expanded through endless love
You squeezed blood from bone and sacrificed your ego
until you died and resurrected fully naked and healed
You revealed to the world that if we gave ourselves permission
to disenchant from the lie that we are unworthy
to break free from the energetic chains
that bind us to limitation and loops of misery
we would return to oneness and wholeness within ourselves
You shower your love over the world
and flap prodigious wings that blow harmonic winds
that lead lost souls home

You found yourself fumbling and sliding
along the muck and mud of your failures and regrets
Congratulations for coming back home
and reclaiming your sovereignty!
You overcame the abuse by believing in yourself
You conquered your fears and are standing here today
sharing your testimony of how you gave yourself a chance

to forgive and love yourself freely
How I've missed you
long lost friend, my eternal self!
I've mourned for your return
along the patterns of our bones
until we finally found our way home

Remember the steps you've taken
The wins and losses
The triumphs, victories and defeats
They all were the prints
that led you to your healing
Give yourself permission to pace forward
You didn't just find happiness
You tapped into peace
Now you love yourself
unapologetically
and unconditionally
With your ability to yield your mighty power
you proved that love is the way back home

Honey,
you run from your past
as if you haven't lived it.
You race towards your future
as if it's leaving you behind.
You cry as if time is laughing
and clowning in your face
for all the times you rushed
and pushed yourself away.

You are the bridge that unites
the gap of the past and future.
Your present is a reflection
of the best and worst of both.
The time is now to embrace yourself.
You are everything you need to be
right here and right now.

If they say that you are too loud
or outspoken,
ROAR LOUDER
Shake them up with your voice
Let the stories of your pain
rattle them deaf
Make them face the blood they've shed
Brush off their disappointments
from your shoulders
and dance yourself back to peace

-They will harm you no more

Solar Plexus Affirmations

On a Sunday when the sun is at its peak, cleanse a yellow glass candle with Florida water. Light the candle and recite these affirmations out loud:

I am empowered through my connection with the sun.
I am safe to be authentic.
I am bold and courageous.
I am radiant and confident.
I stand strong and firm in my power.
I control my own actions.
I fully trust myself and my capabilities.
I creatively co-create my reality.
I believe in myself and know that I am successful.
I am firm in my truth and express myself authentically.
I stand in my truth with confidence and conviction.
I wisely yield my power for myself and humanity.
I am aware of myself and others around me.
I give others space to express themselves.
I welcome in divine love and warmth.
I am abundantly successful.
I am fulfilled.

KaSandra Turner

You are so magical
and mysteriously omnipotent
How is it that you exist
as a witch, empress
prophet, prophetess
angel, demon
nebula, galaxy
and a portal
all in one?

Divine Healing Ritual

Tools:
Glass bowl
Matches or lighter
Small wash cloth or linen
White seven-day glass candle

Dried Herbs and Resins:
Bundle for smoke cleansing
Chicory root
Echinacea
Frankincense resin
Jasmine Flowers
Juniper berries
Lavender
Myrrh resin
Rosemary
Tobacco/cigar

Salts:
Dead sea salt
Epsom salt

Waters:
Alkaline or spring water
Florida water cologne
Holy water

Oils:
Divine Healing Ritual Oil
Frankincense and Myrrh
Lavender

The Ritual

On a Monday evening, start off your healing ritual with a shower. Visualize your energy being cleansed as you bathe your body. After you shower, run a bath and add Epsom sat, dead sea salt, lavender essential, frankincense and myrrh essential, and a brew of lavender, chicory root, and echinacea. Soak and visualize a white light surrounding you. You may speak prayers, spells and or affirmations for protection.

Cleanse your sacred space with the with the smoke of herbs (preferably ones that are not endangered like cedar, rosemary and mugwort). Invite in your guides, and or ancestors into the space through prayer and or invocations. Gather a glass bowl filled with spring or alkaline water. Add holy water, Florida water cologne, dried chicory root, dried jasmine flowers and rosemary. Bless the water mixture through prayer or by reciting Psalms 51 from the Bible. Cleanse a white seven-day glass candle in the blessed water with the cloth. Gather a pinch of dried lavender, chicory root, crushed frankincense resin, echinacea, and five juniper berries. Awaken the spirits of the herbs and flowers by burning tobacco smoke over them. Thank them for their presence and for granting their healing energy. Add them to the candle. Take a healing oil and add drops in three circular motions. Light the candle and say this prayer into the flame:

Ancestors/Guides (or state the name of a specific ancestor or deity) who faithfully watch over me, I thank you for your benevolent love and divine protection. I resort to your guidance with a humbled heart and an open mind so that healing may find its way to me. My tragedies have been great, and my suffering has been long. I call upon divine healing for my mind, body, soul, and spirit, so that they may be aligned once again. I offer this divine healing fixed candle with herbs and flowers to you every Monday so that I may be healed and whole once again. Lead me to my own divine light that nourishes my spirit and help me to conjure my strength. (State what you are wanting healing from next). Peace has evaded me, and I am calling my power back here and now. Please cover my crown with your higher wisdom and cloak me in your everlasting love. And so it is.

Honor your guides out loud three times: *Ancestors (or) guides I honor you to the highest degree and declare that my steps are divinely guided, guarded and protected. And so it is.*

Call in healing three times again out loud: *Ancestors of love and benevolence who linger through my blood, whose lights are graceful and pure, help me to heal and restore my soul. Smite the trauma(s) that weigh(s) on my heart so that healing and peace is mine once again. And so it is.*

Sit and meditate for eleven, twenty-two, or thirty-three minutes and imagine a green light entering your heart. Chant, *I am healed, restored and at peace.* Snuff the candle out every Tuesday rising and relight every Monday evening for a total of seven weeks.

There were moments I was afraid
of losing my life
because men grew angry
at what they believed to be
my unattractiveness
Some were repleted with displeasure
when I turned them away
Men uninvolved
would pull out their folded seats and popcorn
to enjoy a show
that could lead to my emotional debacle

Women would wrap
their skin and bones around me
They would form a fort of protection
against the wrath of these fools
I was safe in the arms of my sisters
They reminded me of my power
and I thank them for showing me
what it means to be a unit

You protect the women you find attractive
yet leave the ones you find physically grotesque
to fend for themselves
You remind me of a wreaking must
covered with Axe cologne
We can smell your odor
from a planet away
The harsh truth is
that you protect the *pretty girls*
because to you they are soft and feeble
Gullible enough to let you in between
to cream and leave them dry
You are not led by your intuition
but by eyes sunk into an illusion

You open your ribs for your brothers
who rape our bodies and suck our emotions
like the breasts you wish you had at six months
all to leave us like worn down clothing
after you've cut and ripped holes out of us
You build a throne for the ones who beat us
with their words and fists
I wonder where you learned this from

Is this a result of slavery lingering
within your subconscious?
When will you and your boys
have these conversations?
When will you begin
to hold each other accountable?

KaSandra Turner

I have experienced you
deem us bitches and sluts
when we don't respond to your barks
and say no to your sexual urges

We resemble your mothers and sisters
yet you *still* choose to hate us
as if we do not spit you out
from the lips between our legs
We will not stand for your betrayal
or perpetuate your rape culture
Cause whether you can conjure
a hard on or not
our lives still matter

-You need to have those conversations

You embrace and welcome the girly girls
who wear dainty earrings
and aesthetically pleasing press on nails
as sisters and long-lost friends
Yet the ones you believe
don't deserve pretty privilege
are outcasts
teased
discarded
and unworthy
as if they are dishonorable
because they don't look like you
You compete with each other
like volleyball and softball teams
only the winner gets the man
who would double dip
between the both of you

You'll be soft and welcome cat calls
from the men you find attractive
Yet the ones you find conventionally ugly
are called creeps and perverts
despite being genuinely polite and respectful
Do you ever stop to think
why this is?
Do you think that maybe it is just
a part of the human experience
to marvel in the looks
of others so deeply
that their beauty excuses
and pardons their sins?

Sisters,
we must hold each other accountable
Check each other with grace and firmness
The only way we can heal collectively
is by welcoming ALL of us
who are loving energy
and have the desire
to heal and uplift humanity

To Help a Mother Heal

I heard the quaking and rapturing
of my mother's voice
as she scorned my brothers
Her unspoken doubts and sins
diced the insides of her cheeks
as she spit those swords out
I was jabbed and stabbed, but did not bleed
I stared into the pain that confronted me
and kissed it
I told it to wait a day
To simmer and soak in the blood of peonies
I would return to set it free

I expelled the acid that consumed my insides
It was too weak to leave burns behind
I returned to the suffering that hissed at me
Out emerged an epiphany
I undressed myself of the armor
that kept her out
I removed the helmet that hindered
my ability to perceive the love she gave
We peeled the layers of our wounds off
and sat still at her feet
It was the first time I heard
the beauty of thunder
and saw wonder
when lightning struck
Our silence was the invitation
she had never been gifted

We swam into her depths
and saw the shipwrecks
of those who strived to conquer her
We saw the bullet holes and cuts
she had hidden beneath the layers of her skin
We embraced her tears and pulled her in
She had finally exhaled and breathed
She cried out the suffocating debris
of the fires that burned
her gardens away since sixteen
She roared out her pain and we gave her grace
Trust was redeemed
Healing found its way through the door
She showed softness and love once more

Unhealed parents, I cannot tell you the ins and outs of your past and the traumas you experienced. I cannot fully understand how you felt having your backs broken by the hands of those you trusted. Your pain is seen through your children's whimpers and cries when you release and purge your past on their skin. You subconsciously create a barrier that encloses them in the memories of your wounds of abandonment and neglect.

Abandonment and neglect are not only reflected in the tangible ways parents provide for their children. It is in the moments when your child asks for a hug, and you scream for them to sit down when you're steeping in the boiling memories of your own childhood traumas. Your babies are reflections of you; they are showing you everything you were at their age. At times you feel they test your patience, but they are showing you where your parents failed you and how you can shape a new reality for you all. They reveal where you need more grace for others and yourself.

They do not cry because they wish to vex you. They call your name a million times because they trust YOU to care for them in the way they need. Everyone else is simply unworthy. You are the chosen one to guide them through this playing field. They need you in this life because you are their teachers. Are you teaching by inflicting trauma or by embracing and honoring their needs?

Most importantly, you matter just as much as your child does. For without your own balance and effortless harmony, how can you properly show up for them or anyone for that matter? Take several moments to stop and breathe whenever you can. Eat. Buy that coffee. Buy that book. Watch that movie. Cook your favorite meal and be honest if you are asked if you need help. Sacrifice is not what parents exist for. You are your own individual person; divorce the idea that your life must be dedicated solely your children. Having this mindset can cause people to feel resentment towards their own creations. Give yourself more grace. More love, patience and call in the things you need to be successful. You pray for your babies and the Divine hears you. Remember to pray for yourself as your ancestors have for you. And even when you cannot hear the wind or see it move the leaves on trees, it is there. You may not be aware of the prayers being spoken over you, but they are there. *Your babies pray for you.*

Your children may have grown, and it may be time to have those conversations. Apologizing for your faults does not invalidate your own experiences and gaslighting them does not dissolve or conceal your past actions. When they speak up to you and advocate for themselves, it is not disrespect. They are paving a path for the healing you did not initiate. They are not slaves and you are not slave owners. Release this mindset. You are safe to thrive. Trust and know that beneath their need to heal themselves they more than likely yearn to heal and strengthen their bond with you. They love you.

Furthermore, when you apologize to your young, teenage and adult children, you hold yourself accountable for your mistakes while simultaneously welcoming healing for you all. Avoiding to acknowledge and vocalize these crucial truths is a lazy and reassuring route to suppression, guilt, disharmony, disease, imbalance and suffering. Show them you love them in the ways they need. They love you and are learning from you. Single parents: you are seen, loved and understood. Continue showing up for yourself and your children in the best ways you can. They will grow up one day.

-Have the conversations.

There will be days where you'll just sit and stare into the vast space of nothingness. You'll simmer in an overwhelming pool of anxiety as you interstellar travel through the memories of your past trauma. You'll blink and the tears will storm down your cheeks as you ask yourself, *why me?*

There may be days where you'll find your throat roaring as you question the reason your life has unfolded the way it has. Why people treat you with such disgust and disrespect. You'll fall into a tidal pool of questions that reveal your agonizing need to give without reciprocity. You'll wonder why you gave your all only to be gifted agony and despair in return. You'll feel weaker and more overwhelmed as each tear evades your eyes.

The moment you decide you've endured enough suffering will be a profound moment of evolution. You'll understand that suffering is a result of revisiting those tormenting memories that you've attached yourself to. Those memories had power over you because you surrendered yourself as a victim in those moments. You'll realize that the moments you want to cave in are opportunities for total release and surrender.

The moment you decide to release your attachments you will have opened the floodgates of healing, new passions and miracles. Divine light will have a way to flow into your life because you declared that healing and love is your right to experience. Remember that miracles are manifestations that we didn't believe could exist. Know that regardless of our limitations and beliefs that there is no end to the possibilities that have the potential to exist.

Every ounce of sorrow, sadness, anger and rage are valid because they are a part of your shadow. Honor these feelings. When you recognize, acknowledge, and honor them, you honor the shadow. Doing so declares you whole. We must also keep in mind that guiding these emotions and analyzing our feelings through reason and rationality is essential to prevent unnecessary suffering and chaos. Your emotions are fuel for your magick. Implement them in your rituals and ceremonies. Lastly, transmuting these intense emotions is a guaranteed way of raising your frequency so high that nothing outside of you will harm you. This is a promised path to love, peace. And tapping into your full power.

You are worth every ounce and inch of support, healing and love you need. It is your right to live the life that YOU choose. You do not need to comply with or domesticate yourself into a society that does not honor your distinct uniqueness. Set yourself free.

You are here and are chosen for something. No one else will ever do what you do. So, give yourself a chance to show up beyond your limits. You are worth more than living in a feedback loop of survival. No more striving. We are THRIVING from here on out.

You are loved, seen, appreciated and validated. May healing make its way to you.

Have the conversations. Do the workings and be consistent with your rituals. Honor yourself by setting boundaries and holding yourself accountable for your participation in your own suffering and that of others. Healing is impossible without you. Most importantly: *be your own advocate.*

241

Your identity consists of your own individuality and leads you to the authentic blueprint of your soul's mission. Each of us, in our own uniqueness, contains an internal compass that leads us to our ultimate truth and helps us navigate towards our true nodes. That true node is the North Star that leads us back into the hands of Source.

You convinced yourself
that there is no way out of your own mind.
You are right
because you *are* a mind.
A soul here to experience love and fulfillment.
You are here to use your gifts
to help heal the world.
To awaken the masses with your presence.
Trust yourself and share your talents.
For when you do,
you show us how to be
better souls.

The sting from a bite into
sweet and acidic pineapple.
The juice gliding down my chin
as if I was never taught to eat.
The remains of mangoes
snuggled safely between my teeth.
Water creeping on the shore
and chasing my toes.
Seagulls souring and calling out
on the search for scraps.
A spring of sunshine
falling onto the heads of azaleas.
A glass cup of handmade lemonade
mixed with honey and zest.
A hug from an elder
or a childhood friend.

These moments remind me
that this life is temporary,
a flicking flash of light.
That each moment will become a memory,
a moment in time fluttering by.
I choose to immerse myself
in the smallest moments of tranquility.
I will love and be fair.
This is my agreement.

A Reminder When You're Healing

When the quest to healing becomes arduous
and you become cemented by your doubts
remember the power of grace and compassion.

You extend your heart to those worthy and those not.
This confuses me. —*You are worthy,*
yet you over pour for the sake of people pleasing
as if healing is off limits to you.

Your past mistakes are distant footprints
that leave a trail of distressing memories. Let them fade.
They are not meant to hold you hostage
from your future. —*Let go.*

Grace and compassion are steps
that lead you to wholesome healing.
They are the pillars that hold you up to be filled
with the golden flowers of God.
You are the accomplishment, trophy and prize.

Remember that gifting yourself grace and compassion
is an essential part of your passage to peace.
It will welcome an experience opposite of your suffering.
Practice them, for they may not come easy.
It will be splendid when you can finally breathe again.

KaSandra Turner

Your candles and incense
resins and herbs
essences and cleansing waters
are tools that help you
tap into the energy of the elements
They are essentials for spiritual hygiene
and keep you connected to divine forces
They serve you to ensure
you are at your best
What happens when the last incense smokes
the last candle burns
the waters run dry
or no crystals can be found?

The answer is simple
You *are* the embodiment
of these elements
For when you breathe
your lungs expand with life
Your vessel is the earth
that protects and supports you
Fire flows passionately through your blood
Water is the essence of what and who you are
Free yourself from the mindset
that you must consume to be spiritual
Your spirit is the breath
that keeps your body alive

To be an embodiment of these elements
is to be whole
You are whole and you are God

The Magick of Healing

I rinsed my sins a thousand times
under a thousand red moons
I tossed runes to divine the reasons
I failed to reach a tranquil state of divinity
I stormed agony from my throat torched
with thunder forged from the pits of my past selves
I dwelt in skins burned, bruised and withered
by the winds of my lost sentiments

I prayed for the day I awakened
to a new pair of all seeing eyes
to see the light I snuffed within me
I became my own worst enemy when I believed
that anyone could ever know me
love me, touch me or honor me
the way I do with a better mind
a better heart, a softer pair of hands
and a pair of knees strong enough to bend
deep beneath Earth's crust to meet her core

Here I am now, eyes glittering and glistening
through my mirror as if roses could be seen
peeking through my bronze cheeks
As if dust never touched my windows sills
As if I arrive home to a shrine of white candles
and buttered bread blessed by the great Mother Mary herself

Here I am now, mimicking a rising lotus flower
untouched and untainted by the filth of life's muck
Here I am, dazzling and radiant as ever
catching petals as they fall
because there is beauty in shedding layers
should we choose to sprout again

A Simple Spell for Healing

On a Monday, cleanse a pink candle with a mixture of Holy Water,
Florida water, chicory root and rosemary. Light the candle and
recite three times:

My heart is true and filled with grief
I call the divine to set me free
Let love be here and fill this room
Free my mind from eternal doom
Heal my heart, mind and soul
Remove the hurt that prevents my glow
Thy power is great, I trust in thee
this spell is cast
So let it be!

Solitude is Good to Me

Solitude is good to me.
She bows to me in silence
and allows my ears to heal
from the bleeding blackened blisters
of my eardrums
that were beaten by the batting noise
of my chaotic confusion.
She hears me when
the mouths of my torments
sing and drown out messages
the heavens leave.

Solitude is good to me.
She honors my privacy
to drown in my tears
of past guilt and shame.
She made a redbrick walkway and a bench
for my ancestors
to sit beside me, silently.
I can feel my body better
when solitude enters the room.

Solitude is good to me.
She is strict. No masks are allowed
on her sacred grounds.
Restoration is inevitable, a nonnegotiable.
A peaceful route back to me.
Empathy and patience become me again.

Solitude is the right place
to connect authentically
to the god in me.
I am grateful for solitude.

The Purging

The purging was not to throw knives
at the necks of your oppressors and abusers
It was not to choke them
with the chains of your angst and fears
If it was, may it have been in the name
of balance

The purging was to free yourself from their grips
To release yourself from the sound
of blades fiercely gliding against concrete sparking
flames that burn holes in the doors
of your mind

The purging was the result
of your dedication to heal
through endless nights of ceremonies
where all you could feel
was the crushing pressure of defeat and sadness
flooding in on you

The purging was the final act
Before cracking open to reveal
what needed to be poured within you
It was breaking free of all things
that no longer served you

KaSandra Turner

The Burning

The eternal fires that raged throughout your body
did not burn to leave you to muck
They did not wish to send your soul away
from the remains of decayed flesh
with no traces of your existence

They heard you bemoan
the demise of your innocence
They heard your laments
to be reborn with skin
that could withstand the strongest tantrums
of a thousand gods

The fires that forever burned
as you were chained to that lifting bed
unsupported by gravity,
was a crucial part of a ritual
Those fires were cleansing your soul
of the laughing fears, doubts and screams
You were baptized in the heat of your passions
Your soul knew
that a resurrection was long overdue

Your soul performed the greatest act of alchemy
It transmuted your pain into desire, into beauty
Just look at you,
radiant with a fluorescent aura
Untouched and not phased by your past
You have risen from the infinite bliss of horror

251

The calming rivers of your eternal love
await to wash you clean

In a world where you are told who to be
how to be, what wear and what to think
remember that seeds contain
all the information needed
to grow into shrubs, flowers
fruit and trees.
Under the perfect conditions
they will grow authentically.

You are a growing seed
with everything that you need
already within you.
Stretch your stems
and raise your petals.
Boldly share your beauty
and with your own permission!

I peek through my window and find the stars
dancing and cheering us along.
We have been stabbed
with the pitchforks of our traumas.
We were widowed before our thirties
and have a past filled with beatings, blood and tears.
Look at us now,
in love and giving ourselves another chance!
I admire us; I'm struck in our brilliance.

-We discovered other reasons to live again

Like water, I cleanse and flow
Like earth, I adapt and sculpt
Like fire, I am bold and passionate
Like air, I am swift...
I am free

Crown Chakra Affirmations

On a Thursday evening, cleanse a purple candle with Florida water and the smoke of Palo Santo. Light the candle and recite these affirmations out loud:

I am one with myself and universal consciousness.
I follow the universal laws to promote peace and balance.
I am divinely connected to ethereal wisdom.
I am rational and use my critical thinking skills.
I trust in my inner knowing.
I trust in the divine wisdom of the cosmos.
I am the universe experiencing itself.
I express my inner wisdom through my art.
I share my art and wisdom with the world.
I am open to receiving guidance from trusted sources.
I apply my knowledge in a way that supports my purpose.
I am purposeful in my actions daily in abundance.
I honor my divinity and that of others.
I am connected to myself and all life on the planet.
I am connected to my ancestors and spirit guides.
I am compassionate with myself and others.
I transcend beyond my pain and suffering.
I am aligned, balanced and whole.
I am love.

Greatness is a byproduct of an individual expressing their authentic identity. To achieve greatness, one must do the unthinkable act of tapping into their own spiritual power and natural talents. They must deconstruct and regurgitate who they've been molded to be. Their character must effortlessly emulate the wonders of the universe.

Sometimes our tragedies are the triggers that jump start our awakenings. They are the initiations that some of the strongest healers experience to step into their higher purpose. How can we truly know peace if we cannot attest to having experienced the currents and tsunamis of life? How can we truly know our power if we are not faced with moments where our power is needed?

You have suffered because you are a healer. You are the medium between the physical and ethereal. Since you have known pain, you must also know pleasure. You have experienced lack. Now you must experience prosperity. You are a magnificent guide here to help the world become balanced and restore peace on this planet.

Your strife has not been in vain. I see you. Your tribe sees you. This world is brighter with you in it.

Self-care magick does not always look like casting spells directly out of a grimoire or partaking in guided ceremonies. It looks like waking up, brushing your teeth, showering, washing your hair with shampoo infused with your intention oils. It looks like a hot cup of hibiscus and cinnamon tea dazzling with sweetener. It sometimes looks like casting a spell that says, "No." It looks like not overexplaining and keeping your energy to yourself.

It is essential for the soul to thrive and evolve in this realm. When you devote yourself to caring for your spiritual body you will welcome healing in all aspects of your life.

Keep up with your spiritual baths. Burn your incense. Charge your crystals under the moon and pull cards for journal prompts. Whatever keeps you in alignment must be a priority.

YOU are the priority and it's okay to give yourself permission to be so. Work your magick in a way that suits you.
Oh, yes! One last thing...

You ARE the magick, you spiritual badass!

I've got armies of ancestors in my cells
Their sacred knowledge runs through me
Who are you to fix your staff and lips
to ordain me as a priestess
prophetess
wisewoman
witch
lightworker
when my spiritual path does not depend
on your magick?
I was born for this life
and you will control your ego
because whether or not you believe in me
I am aligned in my divinity

KaSandra Turner

I love to see your natural skin
The wrinkles under your eyes remind me
of rippling water in a pond
Your laugh lines are proof
that there is joy, pleasure and play in this life
Your textured skin reminds me
of the soil that protects seeds I plant
Your eyes glow so brightly
that the sun will move and hide behind clouds
so that a shadow is cast over your lovely face
He'll move in regret
eager to witness those brown eyes again

Your lips are pink petals
that press gently into each other
Is this what two hearts look like
when they are sandwiched together?
Your pores are open to the pollen flying
off the cute butts of bees
Your brown skin emulates the beauty
of trunks on mysterious trees
I enjoy seeing you enhanced
with makeup that glamours your natural cheeks
I really love it when
you wear your own skin
It's an organic beauty pageant
Untouched and undefined
It is a testimony that
even the softest parts of us are resilient

They stabbed your insecurties on a hook

to bait you into consumerism
They feasted on the shell
of your authenticity
you traded in and left behind
I'd rather you let your skin sing
and honor your natural beauty
It is when you are in this state
that I can truly see you

KaSandra Turner

The earth opened herself up
and I curled into her womb
in fetus position
to be protected, nurtured and reborn
I grew into the most amazing flower
that bees and butterflies fly around constantly
They pause to take a good look at me
and soak in a moment of my presence
They flutter and fly away in awe, astonished
that the earth could grow
something so breathtaking and unique

I have returned home to my body
my mind
my spirit
after a life of tragedy and tears
I can finally say that my rituals paid off
I am finally in the space
that I've always wished to be

Life is like a Ferris wheel
There are moments where I'm elevated
and can see beyond the Eye of Sauron
There are moments where I am so low
that I can smell the fumes
of El Diablo's burnt brick floors

I choose not to react to my lows
or soak too long in my highs
I choose to respond and appreciate
my ability to flow with wisdom

-Wheel of Fortune

Healing is in the breath
that awakens the lungs
Healing is in the tears
that cleanse the mind
Healing is in the passion
that charges the soul
Healing is in the vessel
that protects the heart

Healing is in the laughter and the anger
The failing, falling and succeeding
Healing is more than just dreaming
It is a journey that gives life meaning
Healing is necessary
to thrive on purpose

I love to see strangers
giggle at restaurant tables
as their metal forks bounce
off freshly cleaned carpets
I marvel in the laughter of strangers
as they pace down the sidewalk
falling over from corny jokes
I love the sound of airplanes
roaring through the clouds
while bicyclists claim the streets
ringing their bells for pedestrians to make way
Children chasing down trucks for ice cream
like it's their last junk supper of a lifetime

I love to see humanity in harmony
Our unity inspires love and prayers
to emerge from beneath my tongue
I pray that one day we will turn to each other
smiling and squeeze each other's hands
unite and reclaim our right to exist in peace
May we always choose healing
and show one another our front teeth
instead of bullets, machetes and pitchforks
Let's lift our eyes away from their tricks
and return to the balance of universal love

May our self-hate become worldly love
our weaknesses become our strengths
and our insecurities become our lessons.
May what keeps us separated
become what unites us
all in the name of balance.

-We are stronger as a unit

I enter my prayer room, this time with smiles and a light heart. I find the sun peeking through my curtains. I pull them back to find him smiling so brightly that the love he pours on my brown skin slightly stings. My crystals sing and plants dance to their melodies.
I take a white candle and cleanse it in spring water, holy water, Florida and rose water. I say a loving prayer of gratitude to my guides and higher self. I place frankincense, myrrh, red clover blossoms, rose petals and mugwort into the candle and add a few drops of my custom made healing oil. I bless the candle, light it and place it in the middle of my altar.

This candle burns to heal me of all the things I keep in secrecy out of shame and lack of self-worth. As it burns, I unravel and bleed out the remainder of toxins that keep me away from my divine purpose. I release the need to be overly critical of myself and cut the cords to people and habits that I allowed to make me feel inadequate. As the candle burns, I stare into the flame and am flown into my memories. The visions play like a compilation of my most vulnerable moments where I poured my heart out for healing and acceptance.

After the painful memories shed their skin, I am shown visions of moments at my happiest. I see me for who I am now: a beautiful woman wise in her power and gives abundantly to help humanity heal. I forgive myself for the times I abandoned me. For putting others above myself. I gave myself as an offering to those that needed my light when they possessed no true love or interest for me. I was insecure and was ignorant of my own self-worth.

This candle burns to melt away the final layers that cover my authenticity. This candle is a reminder of my dedication to love myself unconditionally. It burns as a reminder of my devotion to heal by working my magick.

When the day falls away, I'll snuff the candle out and continue to burn it every Monday for five final weeks. May the light shine and glisten over the entire world. May my flame be an inspiration to those who choose to heal by working their magick.

The Magick of Healing

It is so peaceful here
The judgments of others are spirits
who have been set free
I am safe in my beauty
as misunderstood as it is
I have bestowed permission upon myself
to exist authentically
Worry no longer anchors me
to limitation or unworthiness
I have risen above the outdated belief
that relief must only come
when their thoughts come stumbling in

I am so in love with myself
that even the stars are inspired to shine brighter
The majestic monarchs clap their wings
as they sore above my sunflower crown
The wind back flips through my curly strands
I can feel Momma Earth's heartbeat again
My quiet tongue, resting forehead
and tears are my testimonies
of surviving my tribulations
Of sacrificing my strength for a moment of belonging
I love it here
cause after a life of loss and limitation
I know, truly
that this is what freedom feels like

This is the magick of healing.

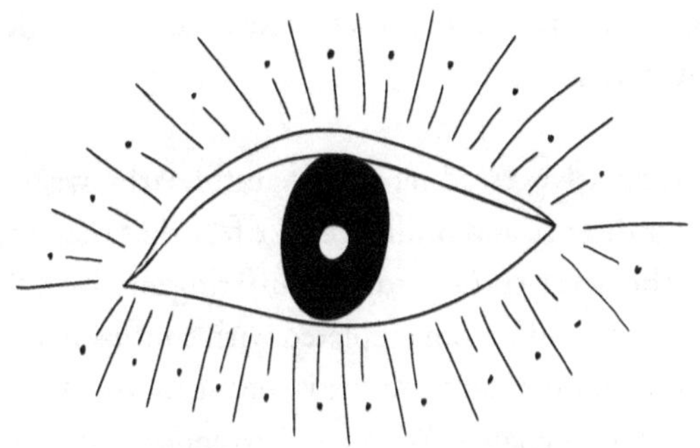

No one heals you.
You choose to heal yourself.

Transformation is the magical process in which we reclaim our power and unfold into the most authentically beautiful higher versions of ourselves. It is the testimony and proof that we trusted in the Divine and our ability to waltz into the unknown, thus creating a magical life with the purest intention.

When we find ourselves treading along painful paths, we sometimes forget our magnificence and brilliance. We fear that the other side may be filled with the never-ending story of suffering and lack. We sometimes question our worth and become repleted with confusion and cling to the idea that nothing more than suffering is meant for us. We bask in the lie that things just won't change. When we surrender to the solar winds of change, however, and we allow ourselves to fully unfold magic takes place. We become ambrosial beings that change the temperature and frequency of any room we step into. Others cannot overlook or ignore such a magnetic force of love.

When we stand fast and allow ourselves to bend in the harshest storms like palm trees, we sprout, grow and bloom into physical embodiments of celestial radiance. With every tear shed we release crushing wounds and uncertainty. With every deep breath we welcome the newness of life. With every bold step we take we shiver off the old layers of our incapacity. We become freed from the fears of inadequacy and unworthiness. We no longer view mountains as obstacles, but teachers that show us the power of remaining grounded as our points reach towards the heavens. The challenges we faced and what we believed to be defeats were moments where check ins were needed. They were reminders that immersing ourselves in the sweet scents of our floral accomplishments were needed.

Remember that the cosmos is merely a starting point of your infinitely wonderous mind. You are an astounding soul here to remember itself and are accompanied alongside other star seeds who wish to shine home with you. Your individual uniqueness is your truest identity. Allow your voice and art to be the advocate for your authentic individuality. Declare yourself baptized and clean of the gunk and filth that keeps you bound to despair and poverty.

Furthermore, wisdom can be found in the darkest and most unexpected places. In your pain, play, laughs, hurt, anger, rage and silence. Wisdom will always be the gentle guide that awaits you. It takes the form of a mother, friend, cousin, neighbor, a child and even the stranger that shares a simple smile.

Remember your kindness and grace. They are free gifts that can be given at any moment you choose. You are eternally evolving and unfolding. I wish you divine clarity, understanding and love as you embark on this extraordinary voyage to fulfillment, wholeness and healing.

May you always be rational and choose love.

-KaSandra

Meet the witch, author & poet.

KaSandra was born in the loud, fast paced Los Angeles in California Republic. She is an American poet who merges the arts of poetry and magick to bring healing to herself and her soul tribe. She serves others through her endless creativity and intuitive gifts and talents. KaSandra's work is distinct and unique; she leaves traces of occult knowledge, spells, and rituals throughout her poetry to keep her soul tribe engaged and in a deep state of exploration and mystery. She has been an intuitive since she was little girl, wise beyond her years and effortlessly embodies elder-like energy in a sophisticated, graceful, sexy, and mysterious way. KaSandra has an online metaphysical shop where she sells handcrafted spiritual essentials needed for setting intention and ritual magick. She offers intuitive services including tarot readings, dream interpretations and more.

KaSandra wrote, illustrated and self-published her first book Eden: Reclaiming Your Divinity through Poetry and Self-Expression in April of 2021. Her work encompasses suffering, loss, trauma, healing, spirituality and alchemy. She is notoriously known for finding wisdom in the shadows. She guides you on a journey through the dark and leads you to light. KaSandra intentionally shows you through her art that we all can transcend beyond our pain and suffering should we choose a route to healing. Heavily ruled by Jupiter and Saturn, (9th house stellium in the sign of Capricorn, Sag moon and North node in Sag her life has always been about being of service to others through learning and sharing knowledge through writing and witchcraft. She is passionately devoted to serving the world through her work.

KaSandra feels most fulfilled at home, in nature, at her altar and working her magick for herself and the collective. She enjoys chocolate cake and banana pudding. She has a deep love for gardening, large hoofed animals, reptiles and cats. Interact with KaSandra at info@kasandraturner.com.